The
Playgroup
Handbook

THE PLAYGROUP HANDBOOK

Laura Peabody Broad

Nancy Towner Butterworth

St. Martin's Press   New York

St. Martin's Press
175 Fifth Avenue
New York, N.Y. 10010

Type and Composition by U.S. Lithograph Inc., New York City 10003

1-29-85

Dedication

To our husbands
Russ and Tony

and to our very special
first playgroup mothers
Priscilla Damon and Nancy Keith

Acknowledgments

The ideas of many successful playgroup mothers went into this book and we are deeply grateful to all for their creativity and enthusiasm.

We extend special thanks to Dr. Harriet Hair, assistant professor in the music department of the University of Georgia, Athens, Georgia, for her recommendations on our music sections; to Rita Lynn, who gave us her extensive collection of playgroup materials; and to Dorothy Wignall, who contributed many hours to typing copy for us.

We also thank Fabric Research Laboratories of Dedham, Massachusetts for providing us with a quiet place in which to work.

Contents

Introduction

The Playgroup Handbook is a guide for the mother who is planning a playgroup or dealing daily with her own child and his friends. She will probably not be specially trained to deal with the preschool child, and her facilities will not resemble those of a professional nursery school.

We believe she would like to have a handbook like this, as easy to use as a cookbook on her kitchen shelf. When she reaches for it she will find many projects in a number of subject areas all whittled down to fit the capabilities of her preschoolers. With its help she will be allowed to use her own special talents to advantage and obtain support in areas where she feels less secure. There will be no need for her to spend large sums on special equipment because the emphasis will be on making use of the already existing toys, materials and environment.

The book will take her through playgroup from its organization, as mothers plan over cups of coffee, through the months as the individual mother arranges what she is going to do when it is her day with the children. The collection and use of different materials will be discussed and there will be a sample plan of a playgroup day. Most importantly there are many activities, both seasonal and nonseasonal, to choose from. These activities are arranged in a progression through the months of the year. While many can be used at any time, they are set forth in this manner simply so the mother has at her fingertips concrete guidelines which she can put to use in a flexible way.

While this book is addressed to mothers throughout, there is no reason to limit playgroup membership only to mothers. Where it is possible—where both parents work at home or have flexible schedules—it is marvelous to have playgroup fathers as well as mothers. And don't forget grandparents who live in the same house or nearby! Adults of different sexes and different ages add a dimension to children's experiences that no mothers' group, no matter how varied and interesting, can supply. So if there are other adults in the family who are willing to take the playgroup occasionally, welcome them and encourage them!

Both of us hold master's degrees in education and are experienced elementary school teachers. One has been on the board of a cooperative nursery school for four-year-olds and helped organize a nursery school for three-year-olds. While this is all good background experience in putting together a book such as this, we think our most important qualification is that we both have been and are now playgroup mothers.

The material in the book comes largely from our own playgroup experiences. The activities in large part have been done in our groups. We have supplemented our ideas with those of other playgroup mothers, and have referred to activity books and sought advice from professionals to strengthen specific areas.

A. Preliminaries

The impact of educational television is upon us all. Your three- or four-year-old is full of A-B-C's and 1-2-3's and soaking up every song and fact the media can offer. You want to build on this stimulating foundation and you are aware that your child needs much more than his relationship with the latest characters on educational television. You sense he wants and needs to be with other little people forming social relationships. He could be learning to function in a group situation, perhaps a slightly more structured situation than that provided by the occasional playmate. He really is not ready for nursery school or perhaps there is no nursery school conveniently located for you. Maybe you would simply like to have him at home a little longer before he encounters formal education. Possibly you think that part of the week at nursery school and a day in a home group would furnish an ideal balance.

There are many things to consider. How are you going to make the days you have the group at your home happy, productive and worthwhile for the children and yourself?

Certainly the child exposed to television learning is more advanced than a child of the same age a few years ago. He has been lengthening his attention span; he is being prepared for reading; he has been exposed to many new concepts. Yet it has been a static situation.

In your group you want the children to broaden their areas of awareness through their own experiences with one another. You want them to achieve a sense of accomplishment by *doing* for themselves, and by creating. You want to see their eyes shining as they excitedly show a treasured item with, "Guess what we did today."

You would like a few guidelines on setting up your group, and most of all you would like a myriad of ideas for exciting things to do, so your group can be a really enjoyable growing experience for the children.

This book will give you a few tools with which to work. Of course you will take the ideas and tailor them to your own needs and those of your children.

Selection of Mothers

What mothers will join you in the formation of your group? Jane, who had seven years of teaching experience? Nancy, who was a dental hygienist a year before marrying? What matters is not so much what their previous experience has been but the mutual desire to form the group and a few similar ideas about its goals. There is absolutely no substitute for the enthusiastic mother who is motivated by the love of doing things with and for her own child.

We remember an exuberant mother who bundled a group of four-year-olds into her car and set off for, of all things in New England, a buffalo farm! En route she stopped at a filling station, asking the startled attendant to please fill up the buffalo bus with buffalo gas—much to the delight of the children. Everyone caught the spirit. It was clearly a pleasure to the mother to have it be "her day."

Avoid the mother who is using playgroup purely as a convenient baby-sitting arrangement. Certainly any mother needs and wants a break, but if she is doing it only for a break, her "day" with the children will be a nuisance to her, and the little ones will feel it. She is not likely to plan ahead and is less likely to provide a very happy, relaxed atmosphere for them. She will be the one to cancel out on her turn at the slightest provocation. If you should find you have a mother who refuses to do her share when the group is under way, the wisest move (difficult though it may be) is to politely eliminate her as a participant.

The mothers in your group will have different abilities and interests. Some may even be trained or experienced in a particular field, but this is certainly not necessary. Each individual should capitalize on her own interests—her enthusiasm will be contagious.

One playgroup mother has her father living with her. Time with grandfather in the garden has become a real treat for the children, especially when they are sent home with ripe tomatoes they have picked right from the vine.

Another mother loves walks through the garden of a nearby estate and tramping in the snow by a lake. Her own love for what she is doing makes the children simply glow with the shared experience.

Ages of Group Members

Who should the children be? Emphatically the ideal is to have them the same age. The year between a two-year-old and three-year-old or a three and a four makes a great difference in both interests and attention span. A two-year-old is most content just playing beside a friend. The three is preoccupied with "me" and "mine" and his attention is diverted very quickly. The four can devote himself to an activity with a companion for quite some time. Anyone who has had the same playgroup over a period of three years is amazed at how independent and reliable four-year-olds are in comparison with the threes, who simply fall apart in a group if left unsupervised for a few minutes. Most threes can work at a task only a short time before becoming interested in something else, while the four can tackle a project with some degree of persistence. A ten-minute directed art activity is plenty for many three-year-old groups, but a four-year-old group might be intrigued with some creative undertaking for 20 minutes. Needless to say, there are enormous differences among children. You will get to know your own group and will gear your activities according to their particular needs.

Sex of the Group Members

Some mothers may wish to have an all-girl or all-boy group. At this early preschool age it comes naturally for the children to play with both sexes. As they approach five or six the separation becomes more evident, and boys and girls often prefer different activities. If you have equal numbers of both sexes, the children can have times of happy play together as a group, and, when inspired, the girls can go off for tea party play while the boys spend some time with their trucks and rough stuff. For variety, it is a good idea now and then to encourage the boys to "cook dinner" and other traditionally girlish things, and to suggest that the girls play with trucks and trains.

Perhaps it will be impossible to balance the sexes simply because there are not many young children available to you. It does not make sense to go out of your way for a certain group mixture if you find you have a willing number close at hand.

Size of the Group

In the enthusiasm of planning a group you may find a number of mothers wishing to have their child join. Small numbers are a *must*. Not only is space a factor to be considered, but the average mother will find herself busy, indeed, with just a small group. For three-year-olds, four in a group is large enough. Remember—four easily distracted people are easier to control than six who have begun to get a little wild in a moment of Mother's divided attention. It is amazing the bedlam that can ensue while Mother answers the phone or chats with a neighbor who has unexpectedly dropped by. Even with a small group in her care, the playgroup mother must learn to tell a caller, "I have a playgroup here now. I'll call you back later."

While four in a group is a good number for the younger ones, the four-year-old with his greater independence and longer attention span is easy to manage in a slightly larger group. If there is space available and all the mothers are willing, five or six is a good number.

What To Do with Younger Brothers and Sisters

You have your ideal-aged, perfect-sized group all set up, but what *does* one do with baby sister or brother? If your group is aged three and you have a baby, for the sake of Mother's sanity and the manageability of the group, the best solution is to trade off the younger sibling with another playgroup mother or a neighbor. As we pointed out, the younger group needs your full attention, and that is certainly impossible when a baby is making his demands.

If you have the four-year-old group, you can more easily manage with the younger child, too, though it is not ideal. If the younger child is two or three he can even tag along with the group and join in some of the creative activities working at his own level with Mother's help. In fact you will make out better if he is allowed to join rather than feel pushed aside.

A case in point was almost-two-year-old Neil, who watched at the edge of things as his brother and friends cut and pasted some paper bag puppets. He first cried because he wanted some materials. Denied them, he went quietly into the other room where he reduced the binding and pages of his brother's *Winnie the Pooh* to shreds and threw them at his mother's feet waiting for a reaction. He had reached his peak of frustration and acted accordingly. A few minutes later he was happily hooked into his high chair beside the other children, armed with blunt scissors, a crayon and paper where he stayed content for the next half hour. How much simpler and happier for everyone if he had been included in the first place.

Facilities

Now where should all this productive activity be taking place? It really makes no difference whether you are an apartment-dweller with no garden or a suburbanite with some yard space available. There is no specific house or yard requirement. It is simply a matter of establishing a workable pattern for the space available. A back yard is great to have, equipped or not, but city streets and parks provide endless possibilities for excursions.

Whatever your inside facilities, it is important to decide which room or rooms will be used by the children. Simply see to it that for all the playthings there is a special place, and that when the day begins as well as when it ends, everything is tidily in place. Though there may be dozens of toys in a messy room, somehow disarray confuses young children, and they cannot find anything to do. At the end of a play day, it can be a matter of pride and learning for them, and a help to you, if everyone pitches in to put things back in order. Clearly designate the tasks: "George, put the blocks in this box." "Mary, line up the dolls on that bench." It will be surprising what a good job little ones will do.

It should not be necessary to buy a great amount of equipment for the group. Each home becomes a special attraction because of what it has . . . a slide at one, a hobby horse at another, a dollhouse some-where else. The playgroup mother need not try to create the perfectly equipped professional nursery school. The emphasis should be on making the most of what she already has. Of course, it will be necessary to purchase materials, as the need arises, for special ac-tivities such as arts and crafts.

The playgroup does not always need to meet at your home on your day. Wherever you live there are endless possibilities for trips and outings . . . a picnic in the park or woods, a visit to a museum which has something of special interest for your group, a morning at the local library for story hour—but more about this later.

Planning Your Program

The year will be happier for everyone if the mothers come to some agreement ahead of time about what they expect of one another and what the group's goals should be. One mother may envision a playgroup as being a morning of general free play for the children. Another may desire a structured program in which every mother must plan mornings balanced with a sampling from every subject area and designated times for a rest period and juice. Both of these views repre-sent extremes. You and the other mothers can come to a general agreement about what kind of day you want your children to have and agree to plan your days accordingly. You may settle on a basic plan which all of you will follow, or you may decide that you wish to leave the decision about each day's activities to the individual mothers. The object is to suit the desires and needs of yourselves and your particular group. The section PLANNING A DAY (page 20) may serve as a point from which to work. You can discuss some of the ideas in that chapter and adjust them to suit your own needs. A little planning ahead of time together will save misunderstandings later on.

The Group's First Encounter

Some of the children in the group may not know all of the other children and mothers. While it is impractical to have meetings of all the mothers with their children at each individual house, there needs to be some effort made so the children have at least met all of the people who will be involved. Such an effort is necessary for each child to feel secure as he ventures into new surroundings with new faces in his first experiences away from his mother.

One solution which has worked satisfactorily is to have a special outing for all the mothers and children. One group spent a sunny day picnicking at a nearby beach. After a few hours of splashing and munching sandwiches together, the little ones, as well as the mothers, felt like longtime friends. Your group's outing could be as elaborate as that one or simply a get-together for refreshments and playtime at someone's home.

Special Problems

There are some children who do have a particularly difficult time facing a group when they are away from their mothers. The mother of such an unhappy child may not even be aware that he is having such a miserable time when she is away from him. The other mothers should let her know if there is a separation problem, so everyone can cooperate in helping the child adapt to what for him is a frightening situation. And she could help in a gradual transition by attending playgroup full-time once or twice and then on other occasions staying progressively less and less time before quietly but firmly departing.

If any child has a special fear or problem that might affect his behavior at playgroup, his own mother should let the other playgroup mothers know about it, so they can aid him in working out the difficulty. Problems of this nature can be discussed most gracefully while the playgroup is in the planning stages.

Occasionally there is a child in the playgroup who turns out to be a discipline problem. Talk about this possibility before it occurs and come to some agreement about how you will cope. When you are finally confronted with a severe situation which the normal firm stand does not seem to alleviate, then the most direct approach is to contact the child's mother to enlist her aid. If the communication takes place with an objective attitude of wanting to help, there need be no hard feelings. The mother of the unruly child may have a few practical suggestions.

When the problem is affecting all of the mothers, they can lend one another ideas on how to handle the child. It is terribly important that tact and understanding be the keynotes in working out the solution. The mother of a child who is experiencing any kind of difficulty should never be made to feel defensive.

Safety

Safety requires planning with caution so that the materials used and the way of managing activities insure a safe experience. It also means the mothers should be prepared for the unexpected.

One group may be hyperactive, so you find yourself automatically on guard for the climber who is continually investigating beyond playgroup boundaries, or the experimenter, the daredevil who will attempt anything and winds up needing the Band-Aid treatment. Some groups are low-keyed and easygoing, but this does not mean you can feel completely secure. Often the quiet ones will be wanderers who get lost if left for a minute during outdoor play, or they are the kind to sample inedible activity ingredients without calling attention to their act.

If you have found it necessary to have a younger brother or sister on the scene, the challenge becomes greater. You must be sure of that child's well-being before you become involved with group activities. You need to be aware of what each person is up to at all times. Small children can easily sense the "best" moment for trying the unusual.

Whatever the makeup of your group, avoid mishaps by screening materials for safety, planning ahead so you do not have to leave your preschoolers unattended, establishing appropriate limitations and rules for the group at your home and thinking how you would handle a serious emergency.

To enable you to handle the unexpected:
1. Have these numbers by your telephone:

—Your doctor or local hospital
—Poison center
—Police
—Fire department
—Location of the children's mothers

2. Have a first aid booklet in a very handy spot.
3. Have basic first aid equipment in a kit on the shelf.

Suggested Basic First Aid Equipment

—3"x3" sterile gauze dressings, nonstick, individually wrapped for cleaning and covering wounds
—box of assorted adhesive dressings (Band-Aid, Curad or other similar bandage)
—roll $1/2$" wide adhesive tape
—small bottle *MILD* antiseptic (mercurochrome is fine, and the kids like its color)
—box baking soda (bicarbonate of soda) for insect bites, etc.
—tweezers (for splinters)
—needles (for splinters)
—ipecac (to induce vomiting after swallowing poison)

NOTE: Burn treatment: Submerge injured area in cold water—a burn requiring more involved treatment requires the attention of a doctor.

Remember that when there is an emergency situation you have a *dual* responsibility. You must take care of the child who is in trouble *and* see to it that the other children are not left unsupervised. There are two questions to ask yourself before each playgroup day: Is there someone nearby to call on for help? Is there transportation available?

How Often To Meet

How frequently the group meets will, of course, depend on the wishes of the mothers. Once or twice weekly is enough for the average mother. It may be best to leave the daily situation to the professionals and take the limitations of the housewife into realistic consideration. If the consensus is that more than once a week is desirable, then for the sake of continuity it is best for the mothers to take turns by the week rather than by the day.

While some mothers might prefer an all-day group, including nap times, most will find that breaking up the group by early afternoon is best. The children are surprisingly tired from the stimulation of the morning's activities. There are groups that have functioned successfully both ways.

Transportation

Distance between the children's homes is a consideration. If each is an only child and there is no one else to consider, then long drives are not necessarily a problem. For maximum convenience, however, the closer the better. Each group of mothers will have its own feeling concerning whether it is preferable for each mother to provide transportation on the day the group comes to her house or on other days. It would seem that just planning and overseeing the activities of the day is enough responsibility without the additional task of ferrying people about.

Playgroup is a unique opportunity. Remember that you are not teaching a curriculum or trying to compete with nursery schools. You have the chance to find the best in each child and enjoy him for just that. You will also have the experience of coming to know your own child even better as you watch him participating in a group of children his own age.

B. Gathering Materials and Planning

The mothers have agreed on all the ground rules for the group. The schedule has been decided upon and the car pool worked out. Now it is up to you to carry out plans when your day comes up. You are on your own!

Attention turns to collecting materials to have on hand for various projects. It will be helpful to know what basic items to purchase and what to save for future use. You will also welcome a few hints on how to plan effectively for the children.

Materials

BASIC ITEMS TO CONSIDER PURCHASING

There are a few items which you will need to purchase in order to function. Most of these are for art work. Some may be bought or borrowed as you choose the activities for a new playgroup day. Certain items will be used so frequently that it would be wise to purchase them at the outset. You will find most of the materials you need at hobby shops, stationery stores, five-and-dimes or department stores. The most vital materials will be starred in the following lists.

ART MATERIALS

Painting
*paints
  *powdered tempera (inexpensive, mix to right consistency with
      water. Add a little dishwashing liquid for ease in laundering
      paint-soiled garments—1 tsp. detergent to 1 pint of paint.)
  tempera, ready-mixed, also called poster paint (very expensive)
  finger-paints (ready-mixed or combine liquid starch and powdered
      tempera)
  watercolors (easy to use and clean up)

*brushes
  large easel brushes with long handles and stiff bristles (often called
      kindergarten brushes)
  1" hardware brushes (less expensive and work equally well)
      NOTE: clean brushes in cold water and soap and store in a can or
      wrapped in newspaper.

sponges (for clean-up or sponge paintings)

*paper
  manila, yellow or white (buy in large quantities for economy, divide
      among mothers)
  oaktag
  newsprint for easel or table painting
  shelf paper or fingerpaint paper
  brown paper bags (cut open)
  newspaper (can be used for paintings)
  construction paper (colored sheets)
  gum-backed colored paper
  colored tissue paper (to add a new look to any cut-and-paste activ-
      ity, especially collage)

Drawing
  *magic markers (*wide or thin point)
  *crayons (preferably fat kindergarten type)
  chalk
  *pencil
  pen

Cutting
  *scissors (choice of left- or right-handed, *blunt or sharp end)
  paper punch

Pasting
  paste brushes
  *glue (Elmer's diluted with water is best-sticking, but expensive)
  *shell or small dishes to hold paste or glue

  Paste recipes
  1. *No-cook paste* (not too sticky)
    handful of flour
    pinch of salt
    add water until gooey

  2. *Boiled paste*
    ¹/₂ cup flour
    add cold water until thick as cream
    simmer and stir five minutes
    keep in refrigerator in airtight jar

Fastening
  stapler
  brass fasteners (good for movable parts)
  *tape
    masking (comes in colors)
    decorated gift tape
    cellophane
  clear Contact paper

Modeling
  play dough (crumbles when dry)
  plasticene
  clay, hardening type (fun for keeping finished product, can be
    painted, hardens without heat; hardened form is porous,
    therefore will not hold liquid unless glazed)
  clay (Crayola clay is very pliable)

  Play dough recipes
  1. *No-cook play dough*
    1 cup flour

1 cup salt (does hurt open cuts on children's hands)
enough water to make dough stiff and a little food coloring
Mix the ingredients, adding more flour if dough is too sticky.
Hardened objects may be painted, but they are brittle and
somewhat crumbly.

2. *Quick-cooking play dough*
   1 cup cornstarch
   2 cups baking soda
   Blend thoroughly in saucepan and add 1 ¼ cups cold water
   few drops food coloring
   Cook over medium heat about 4 minutes stirring constantly
   until mixture thickens to moist mashed-potato consistency.
   Cover with damp cloth to cool. Knead as you would dough.

MUSIC

*records (can borrow)
suggested types:
  musical story records
  simple songs
  nursery rhymes
  music to dance to
  music to march to
  music to play rhythm instruments with
*record player (can borrow)
autoharp
rhythm instruments (homemade or bought)
  bought:
    bells, drum, maracas, tambourine, triangle, rhythm sticks
  made:
    metal spoons to clink, oatmeal box drum, small boxes or other
    containers sealed with macaroni or beans inside for shaking,
    wooden spoon rhythm sticks, jingle mitts (December activ-
    ities), tart tin shakers (February activity), tambourines (April
    activity), sand block instruments (November activity), guitars
    (summer activity)

suggested music books:

1. *America's Favorite Ballads,* Pete Seeger, Oak Publishing Company
2. *Fireside Book of Children's Songs,* Marie Winn, Simon and Schuster
3. *Wake Up and Sing,* Beatrice Landbeck and Elizabeth Crook, William Morrow Publishing Company
4. *Mister Rogers Songbook,* Fred Rogers, Random House
5. *Golden Book of Songs*

PHYSICAL EXERCISE

*large balls
beanbags
any special equipment you already have (swings, slide, wagon, tricycles, balancing board, rocking board, hoppity hop, etc.)
Remember local parks and playgrounds—they are equipped.

WOODWORKING

For the most part you will be using items that Daddy already has in his tool supply. The following list is meant as an aid if you need to purchase some equipment and want a guide to the ideal tools.
*hammer—12- or 18-ounce claw hammer (claw hammer *pulls out* nails too!)
*hacksaw—type for 10- or 12-inch blade. Buy blades with 14 or 18 teeth per inch. We think this is the best saw for small children offering a number of advantages: it is sturdy, offers maximum safety, is easier to cut a straight line with, and can be used with both hands, if desired.
*vise—$3\frac{1}{2}$" light duty with swivel base, if available (or use C-clamp)
coping saw—for $6-6\frac{1}{2}$" blades, 15 teeth per inch. Though commonly used for small children, this saw presents the safety hazard of blades snapping. It is also more difficult than the hacksaw to guide in a straight line.
screwdriver—short, stubby one preferable
    or
$\frac{1}{4}$" blade, $6-8$" long

If children have difficulty with a conventional screwdriver, use a
Phillips-head screwdriver
*nails—2d 1" and 4d 1 1/2" common nails
    1" or 1 1/2" galvanized roofing nails
screws—3/4" and 1" #9 steel flathead
*sandpaper—medium or coarse
    (can use flat piece of wood 4"x3"x 1/2" as a sanding block)
file—10" combination shoe rasp
hand drill—eggbeater type with #9 screw bit and/or 3/16" twist drill
ruler
pencil
carpenter's apron—beg or purchase from local hardware store,
    lumberyard, or builder's supply
painter's hats—given free at the hardware store, builder's supply
wood—scraps of lumber
    preferred:
        scrap ends from 2x4 or 2x3 lumber
        soft wood
        wooden lath—1"x 3/16"

WHAT TO SAVE

There is a wealth of materials that cross your threshold in the
course of daily living that lend themselves to assorted creative activities. Most mothers are already familiar with a few tricks for what
to do with a discarded oatmeal box, empty spools or a styrofoam
meat tray. So that you may add to your ready store of ideas, here is a
list of items and possibilities. Some of the suggestions will be familiar,
others unique. In either case you will draw from them for future projects.

1. *juice cans*—decorate for pencil holders; use as paint rollers
2. *baby food jars*—excellent paint containers
3. *cigar boxes*—ask the drugstore to save them; decorate for
jewelry or treasure box
4. *cardboard containers and tubes*—paint and tape together into
recognizable objects or abstract sculpture designs
5. *newspapers*—minimize clean-up, good for finger-paint prints,
papier-mâché

6. *old shirts*—make smocks, let children decorate with designs cut from iron-on tape (they cut, you iron)

7. *shirt cardboards*—looseleaf books, flannel-board stiffening

8. *paper bags*—for collecting treasures and taking home finished activities *(Put each child's name on his own bag)*

9. *wax or plastic sandwich bags*—used as in no. 8

10. *frozen dinner tins*—compartments lend themselves to paints or sorting trims

11. *styrofoam meat trays*—make substantial Christmas ornaments and also are fun to break up and create 3-D designs with toothpicks

12. *props*—for a "pretend box" including dress-ups and accessories for role playing as doctor, plumber, spaceman, etc.

13. *old wallpaper books*—available free when new editions are coming in, good variety of paper for painting, gluing or cutting, great for wallpapering box houses, shoebox dollhouses, etc.

14. *onion bags*—suet feeders

15. *small flowerpots*—use for seed experiments, for gift plants, to decorate as gifts

16. *material scraps*—collages, puppet clothing, burlap or other for stitchery

17. *buttons*—cloth button-book, making pictures by gluing, sculpture

18. *coffee tins, oatmeal cartons*—make musical instruments or containers for toys with many pieces

19. *trims* (old jewelry, macaroni, lace, ribbon, etc.)—decorate valentines, eggs, boxes

20. *miscellaneous objects* (such as curlers, furniture casters, kitchen implements)—for stamp painting, object memory game, blindfold-and-guess game

21. *water play objects*—funnel, measuring spoons, laundry sprinkler, sponges, plastic cups, boats, suction basters, sieves, corks

22. *clothespins*—used as part of musical shakers, for art drying, puppet figures

23. *empty metal Sucrets or Band-Aid boxes*—to decorate

24. *long shoelaces*—spool, bead, shell or cereal stringing, punched hole designs

25. *rubber bands*—for making a cardboard box guitar

26. *candle stubs or paraffin*—leaf-dipping, juice-can candles

27. *empty spice cans*—paint cans, musical shakers

28. *popsicle sticks*—handles on musical shakers or stick puppets

29. *straws*—handles, paint-blowing, glue on paper for three-dimensional designs

30. *large needles* (needlepoint or stitchery needles)—with yarn for stitching and threading activities

Planning a Day

In the most rewarding playgroups we know the key to success has been planning, planning and overplanning—which your little ones should never be pressured by or aware of. The planning is a matter of having ideas and materials at your finger-tips, to be used on a given playgroup day or set aside for another. The choice depends on the immediate needs and moods of the children.

Materials for projects should be prepared and easily accessible. One mother we know lines her things up on trays ready to whisk on the scene when needed. If you are using a record player or other special equipment, have it set up and ready to go. Make sure it is in working order. Balls or other playthings for which you have planned a special game should be assembled so you need not leave the children while you scramble about trying to retrieve the items. If you are an inveterate list-maker you will, perhaps, make out a proposed schedule for the day or just list the different ideas you have.

Why all this? After all, it is not a military campaign you are planning. But remember that brief attention span of your three-year-olds . . . ten minutes, maybe? You need to be ready to move into some new activity quickly as their interest flags. Your four-year-olds are expected to be interested longer, but what if the project you planned just doesn't strike a chord or takes less time than you expected. You need something else in its place. More planning means more flexibility.

FLEXIBILITY is the key word. Your group may be low-keyed one day, quite equal to listening and to doing quiet activities. The same group may have switched into high gear another day and more time outside is in order, or, if that is not possible, then some moving-around activities inside are necessary. Be ready to switch the order of activities to suit the mood of the day or even of the moment. Be prepared to spring into a little exercise period in the middle of an art project before returning to it.

It will be helpful if you take your cue from exponents of the "ed" schools. They preach an activity rule of thumb—"quiet followed by noise; still followed by movement." One automatically sets the stage for the other. After running about a child is ready to sit quietly and listen to a story; after drawing a picture he is all set to use some of his larger muscles.

For a basic idea of what might be included in your day, consider the following: free play, arts and crafts, music, story, juice time, nature or science project, games, time outdoors. That list sounds more intimidating than it is in practice. You would not, of course, do all of those things every time. The idea of having to set up anything scientific or musical may overwhelm you, but overcoming such apparent difficulties is what this book is for. It includes very simple activities, right for the preschooler and right for the average mother to tackle with her group.

Routine Procedures

Possible problems with the members of your group can be greatly minimized by making clear to the little ones just what is expected of them. Where should they put their hats, mittens, boots and coats when they come in? If you haven't a line of pegs or low hangers handy, make use of the doorknobs down a hallway. The children need to know where the bathroom is located, that they can feel free to use it any time, and that you are happy to help them with any problems they encounter in using it. Make clear which room they can expect to go to during the course of activities and which rooms are out of bounds. It will simplify things for you if they know well that a second-floor bedroom area is off-limits or that they must not go outdoors without your knowledge. There are all kinds of little rules that a mother enforces with her own family for her own convenience and which, for the secure feeling of the children, she should spell out. A simple, "That is against the rules here," works all sorts of magic. The children will depend on your doing this. How comfortable they feel will hinge on their knowing the limitations.

You and Your Child

The bravest mother blanches at the thought of having to cope with some uncooperative, overactive or too aggressive child. It may come as a shock, but this child will probably turn out to be your own. Relax! He will not behave at someone else's house in such a fashion. He will store it up and save it just for you.

He is excited to a pitch that the group will be at *his* house and *his* mommy will be "teacher." The other children descend, and he is distressed to find that all this glory includes their being able to use all *his* things. All of his belongings suddenly become important treasures and he is more than reluctant to relinquish them. Of course learning to share is what playgroup is in part about, but the harsh reality of this can be softened. One way is by suggesting the other children come with a toy. This initially gives them a sense of security, and then as they become interested in your child's toys, he has their toys to examine and play with for some new interest.

Most difficult of all for your child, however, is the fact that he finds he must share *you* with all these people. He may feel called upon to do all sorts of negative things to capture your attention.

Never mind, that same child is going to come home from someone else's playgroup day with the announcement, "David was so naughty that his mommy had to send him to his room." Maybe she even had to carry him there kicking and screaming!

Sample Plan for a Playgroup Day

You may want a concrete plan of attack for setting up your day. Here is a sample plan to give you something from which to work. Essentially all it amounts to is a simple list of ideas of what the mother is hoping to do in a day—a list such as you might scribble in abbreviated form on a piece of scrap paper. Opposite the list is spelled out what preparation is necessary. You might go over your own plans for preparation by making mental notes as you look at your list of ideas—or you might like to jot down a companion list of things you need to do ahead of time in a fashion similar to that shown here.

Following the well-laid plans is an interpretation of how the day actually may have gone. It is important to realize how successful a *rearranged* day can be and that the thoughtful planning and preparation remains the basis for a wonderful playgroup experience.

Sample Plan for a Playgroup Day
(activities drawn from different months)

MOTHER'S PLANS	PREPARATION BEFORE CHILDREN COME
1. Play outside in the snow	

2. Paint in the snow
       or
    do mural inside if
    weather is poor
	2. Mix paint in unbreakable containers a little thick, as suitable for indoor project—to be thinned for the outdoor painting.
	    Put out:
	       shelf paper
	       manila paper
	       scissors
	       paintbrushes (large)
	       newspapers
	       water containers for rinsing brushes

3. Cocoa and crackers	3. Put out:
	       cups
	       crackers
	       instant cocoa
	    Check milk supply

4. Story	4. Put out: book
5. Finger-counting game	

6. Masking-tape game on the kitchen floor	6. Put out:
	       masking tape
	       toy cars
	       dollhouse furniture

7. Music—making loud and soft sounds	7. Put out: "instruments" for music game

8. Cut day-old bread,
   bologna and cheese
   with cookie cutters

9. Lunch—menu
   bologna and cheese
   carrot strips
   bread and butter
   applesauce
   milk and cookies

10. Have every child choose
    favorite toy to play
    with until mother comes
    for children

11. Have "fill-in" activities
    handy

8&9. Check refrigerator for
     luncheon items
     Prepare carrot strips
     Set out:
       cups (paper?)
       plates
       spoons
       cookie cutters

10. Tidy the playroom, make
    sure parts of games and
    toys are together

11. Put out:
      paper and crayons
      simple sticker book
      (a page torn out for
      each child)

As it has been pointed out, plans do not always materialize as you had anticipated. Here is an idea of what might happen to the preceding carefully-thought-out plans.

What Might Happen

It rains—so there is no playing or painting outside. The children are in "high gear." Only one displays any interest in painting. The others are given choices of toys right away instead of later. When they are under control the artist is set up with paint and paper to do a single painting. The mural idea is set aside for another time. The mother is, however, prepared for a change of heart by the others.

The rest of the schedule goes pretty much as planned, but one child is more interested in putting together a puzzle than in the music activity. He is allowed to go his own way, *since he is not distracting the others.*

OR

The day is beautiful! The snow is not very wet, so the children's clothes remain dry, making a long stay outdoors possible. The painting is a huge success. One child spatters. Another child draws lines. Someone else does the first letter of his name and puts eyes, nose and mouth on a snowman. It takes so long to remove the children's clothes once they are inside that it is necessary to set aside the story and the tape game for another day.

In both instances the playgroup day has been a success. The mother has been well prepared, but flexible enough to rearrange her schedule to fit the weather and the moods of the children. As a result the children have had a relaxed, unpressured, happy day while learning from a few well-planned activities.

C. Playtime with the Children

Plan so the Children Can Express Themselves Freely

Armed with a few materials and your plans for the day's activities, you are ready to begin working with the children. Within the framework of your plans, your young visitors will have the facility to express themselves. Your reserve of ideas and materials is prepared in advance. You are ready to stand by as a guide and helper for the busy children. You have not created a rigid situation for working with the children. You have merely set the scene so that they can express themselves freely in a creative way and have an enormous amount of fun doing it. If you are inadequately prepared or if you leave your group of preschoolers on its own, you will soon be confronted with decidedly noncreative chaos.

Set Up Materials so the Children Can Be Independent

Plan special activities so that the children can be as independent as possible. If the materials have been set up ahead of time, the children can do an activity on their own and follow right through the clean-up. Once the project is under way, the children are eager. Any distraction—such as that of finding additional supplies—divides attention, mars enthusiasm and spoils results.

Let us look at an art project as an example. The children are to do finger-painting on a formica table top. Each child is supplied with a small plastic squirt bottle filled with liquid starch, a shaker of powdered paint and a wet sponge. They are now ready to proceed independently.

As the children experiment with varying proportions of starch to paint, they have the fun of trying out different designs, enjoying the smooth feel of the paint as their fingers slip over the table top. When they are finished they may reach for the sponge to wipe up the mess, with a little help from the playgroup parent. The understanding of how to use the paint has grown, the results are individual, and each child has done the whole project from the creative beginning to the tidy end.

How To Show the Children How

It is important to spend time introducing a technique or material being used for the first time at playgroup even if you know the children have been exposed to it somewhere else. Certain skills require actual demonstration. For example, children cannot experiment with cutting until they know the proper way to hold a pair of scissors. Helpful hints are in order on how to throw a ball or how to stir the Jell-o mixture without flipping it out of the bowl. You can ask a child who has already mastered a skill to show others how he does it. He will be proud to oblige, and his peers will learn most effectively from his demonstration.

Some techniques lend themselves to individual interpretation and experimentation. An assortment of ideas here is more important than a set way of using tools or media. The way a child manipulates clay, the number of sprinkles he puts on a cookie or the way he moves as he acts the part of a bunny rabbit are purely individual. Rather than acting as a director, you can work beside the children in such situations. Each person absorbs himself in trying out his own way of testing a new experience. One person might copy entirely another's approach, but he is more likely to make his own discoveries while incorporating some ideas from the work of others.

Begin with Simple Things

When working with three- and four-year-olds, simplicity proves to be the best approach in any area. Generally, it is not wise to try more than one new idea at a time. Another day you can reuse the same technique or activity at a more advanced level. For example, the first time the children use scissors the main job will be learning to hold the scissors and trying to make some kind of cut on paper. After a little practice the youngsters will be able to cut across a small piece of paper making scraps. In time, the children can follow a simple outline—circles first, then squares, rectangles or triangles. Once the cutting of simple shapes has been mastered, they can try more difficult cutting projects.

You might introduce a technique by doing a one-step activity on playgroup day. The next time the children come you might do the same thing but add other steps. An illustration of this is cookie-making. For the first venture, the group might just frost and decorate ready-made cookies. If this undertaking proves to be appealing to them, then during the next session they might cut the shapes from ready-made dough in addition to decorating the cookies. An older group might even be ready to tackle the whole process—mixing dough, cutting and decorating.

Understanding Your Group

You will soon become aware of your group's individual needs, interests and abilities. If it seems necessary, make sure there is an alternate way for different children to accomplish similar results. What one child can do with ease, another child may find much too difficult. You might give group members each a page from a sticker book and suggest that they punch out and match pictures of farm animals to an outlined form. One child in the group finds the matching beyond his capabilities. Sticking the figures on a blank sheet of paper would be easier and more fun for him. He might even enjoy adding a few details with crayon.

Your plans for the group may be complicated by an wide difference in the rate various children tackle and complete an activity. It is impossible to make three children continually wait for a methodical and deliberate worker who always takes twice as long. Yet it clearly is important to that child to feel the satisfaction of finishing. A reasonable amount of time should be provided for each activity. Make sure the child who is unusually slow accomplishes enough of the activity and has sufficient materials so he can easily finish it at home on his own.

Every child can contribute to the group in his own special way. As you begin to know what your preschoolers' abilities are, you can choose activities and assign roles accordingly. In a mural project, one child might cut, while someone else pastes, another draws, and an imaginative nonartist tells a story to accompany the completed picture.

As the playgroup day is planned, you include everyone in most activities without forcing a child to do something he strongly disfavors. Most often the role of the observer is taken at music or dramatic play time by the self-conscious child who wants to join in but needs time to watch and know how to go about it comfortably. He has interest and gradually will become involved in the activity, but in the meantime he will appreciate fringe jobs you find for him.

Sometimes a child just wants to play with the toys and rejects most suggested activities. This is natural at the start and time should be given just to playing and getting to know each other. However, as most of the children become more interested in activities, it is important that an individual not be a distraction to the group while he is allowed to play with appealing alternatives. Two children busily engaged in running racing cars over a network of speedways might find it impossible to work up any enthusiasm for making cinnamon toast. Let them continue to play while those interested in cooking make the toast. Perhaps the kitchen crew will share their toast and add to everyone's good time.

Sometimes a simple matter of interest determines whether a child wishes to take part in a given activity. Someone may never be inspired by artsy-craftsy pursuits. It is far better that a person be allowed to choose another kind of activity while the others do the planned project, but be sure to let him know he is welcome to join in if he has a change of heart.

Certain activities like singing require group cooperation, and here an observer can be important as a listener. But to play nearby, even quietly, would be a distraction and unfair at a time when it is important for the group to be a unit.

Many children at this age have an assortment of colorful individual fears which help to govern the degree of their participation. One playgroup mother had armed her children with collecting bags and set out for a woodland walk. A small girl in the group, hanging a bit behind, ventured no more than several yards into the woods and resisted going one foot farther. Who knows the reason why? The mother responded by taking the group into the field at the edge of the woods. The adventurous among them were allowed to go a short way into the woods, while the girl happily played and collected where she felt more secure. The mother positioned herself where she could see all of the children.

Another playgroup child became convinced, with the help of his imaginative friends, that there was a monstrous creature lurking in the basement playroom of one house. No logic could shake his firm belief. The mother arranged to have the planned activities take place upstairs. Free play was allowed both in the playroom and upstairs, so that each child could be where he was most comfortable. By the next visit, the fearful boy had completely forgotten the awesome dangers of the downstairs room.

Do not be startled when one of your little ones displays some very unique sort of anxiety. Do what you can to make him feel happy. Adapt the activity to the situation and rearrange your plans around his fears.

Knowing Your Own Abilities and Limitations

You, too, have your own special needs, abilities and interests. Consider this fact a distinct advantage. Remember to draw on your own natural interests and talents. You are counting on the other mothers to do the same. The result will be a surprising balance in the kind of experiences the children have during the year. You may be discounting the fact that you are a whiz in the kitchen, for example. Cooking projects with the children might become your forte.

Every parent has certain limitations. Do not be afraid to accept them in yourself. There will be days when you find your plans are entirely too ambitious. Neither you nor the children are in tune with your original ideas for the day. The children are overexcited, and you feel irritable. Feel free to readjust your plans. Simplify. Set aside involved projects such as paper-bag puppets or baking crystals. They are better for congenial, relaxed days because they are the kind of activity more likely to stretch patience.

There will come a day when you don't feel physically up to par but not sick enough to cancel the playgroup activities. Rearrange your plans so that the day does not require so much energy.

Have Fun

The most important element in the successful playgroup day is a feeling of plain, old-fashioned fun. Without that you and your little people might just as well have forgone the day. All of the earlier mentioned suggestions on working with the children do contribute toward this end, but more elusive qualities can be equally important in making "fun" happen.

Your attitude is a major factor. Treat yourself to happy absorption in the children. Try to set aside the nagging details of your daily living. Nothing will build your own confidence more readily than your immersion in the spirit of fun.

Do you feel bound by a need to show the other parents you are doing your part by seeing to it that every child has some product to show for his time with you? If a special holiday is coming up, do you feel pressured to center your planning around that time?

So many activities are entertaining and accomplish real learning whether or not they result in tangible products. Remember those children "squishing" paint to produce their own patterns on the formica surface? Nothing remained to take home after clean-up. The children's delight was in the experimenting, and surely they left the project with a new confidence about finger-painting which they would bring to later trials on paper.

Enjoy the freedom to depart from traditional seasonal activities. In midwinter, when the children have been essentially housebound, break free from snowtime-centered activities for a change. Bring good-weather activities inside with a swing hung from a doorway, a slide hitched to set tubs, or a makeshift basement sandbox. In summer, a target contest using snowballs stashed away in the freezer last February can be an unexpected treat. Don't be afraid to be simple and original in working with the children. Above all, HAVE A GOOD TIME!

Hints for Working in Specific Areas

Art

You will understand the individual children much better as they communicate their emotions through art. They can express a mood of the moment or convey how they feel about the world around them in their manipulation of artistic materials. At the age of three or four, they are largely unable to express their feelings with the spoken word. They find enormous relief and satisfaction in working out their emotions with their hands. The *process* through which the child is going is of prime importance. The product itself does not really matter except as an expression of his feelings.

What you see being produced will bear little relationship to your adult, preconceived notions of what a picture or clay figure should be. It will be an enormous temptation to ask, "What is it?" To the child it is perfectly obvious what it is, because it is so much a part of him. He will find your question, phrased that way, hugely unsettling. Inquire instead, "Can you tell me about it?" and the child may take you into his world. In the explanation of his work he may reveal some of his deepest feelings.

If you were not aware of the place of art work in the child's life, you might unwittingly be responsible for a sad error similar to that of a mother who spent time helping in a cooperative nursery school.

Time after time she had seen Tommy come in, settle himself in front of the easel, carefully choose black paint and proceed to make circle after stark, black circle ... clearly scribbling, clearly not developing artistically or any other way. Wanting to help him progress, she approached him and asked, "Why don't you try making something else? That is just scribbling."

Tommy did not make those big, black scribbles any more, but he didn't try to make anything else either. Tommy stopped painting altogether. He didn't touch a brush for the rest of the school year.

What the mother did not know was that Tommy had gone with his family on a trip to New York City. They had driven through the Holland Tunnel, which, from Tommy's point of view, was the highlight of the family adventure. His picture was the picture of the tunnel. Each time he made those big black circles, he was reliving the happy excitement of the ride. If only the nursery mother had opened the way to sharing Tommy's experience!

To the adult eye black was somber; repeated circles were nothing more than scribbling. You want to view the children's work through the eyes of a child, because in doing so you will encourage your preschoolers to express more of themselves. The development of skills in using materials and in creating realistic figures will evolve naturally and at each child's own pace.

It will help if you understand that there are three stages in the development of children's art. The first is the manipulative stage in which the children experiment with the media. This is the time when the children are pouring their concentration into the sensation of clay as it is felt when squeezed through the fingers, the pleasure of watching pieces fall as the scissors snip off bits of paper or the feel of the brush as it spreads paint across the page. Some members of your group will be in this phase when you begin getting together.

Later comes the symbolic stage. This is the phase in which many three- and four-year-olds find themselves. It is at this point that the child draws, cuts or models things that have meaning for him. People begin to resemble people, but key details such as feet or the nose may be lacking. The young artist exaggerates parts which he feels are important and eliminates others altogether.

Three-year-old Laurie, enthusiastic after the first encounter with ice-skating, came home and filled a paper with faces and double lines drawn in various areas and positions to indicate bodies moving. Skates were missing in the picture, as were many other details, but the rhythm of the lines actually gave a wonderful feeling of people skating. To Laurie, the motion and the numbers of people were the important point, and she expressed it beautifully.

Representative work is the last stage. Figures are more nearly complete. They often stand on a base line. Sometimes both the inside and the outside of an object are shown. This last phase is unlikely to be very evident as you work with your young artists, for it is more characteristic of a kindergarten child or first-grader.

Drawing

The children's first experiences with art will probably have been with pencil or crayon. In your work with them it is better to leave the pencil for writing when they are older. Crayons provide a more satisfying means for creating. An occasional page from a coloring book may be given each child, to help develop the specific skill of controlling the crayon and staying within lines, but generally it is preferable to supply blank pieces of drawing paper. The pictures produced in this manner will be truly original.

Have the children tear the paper wrappers off the crayons and encourage using the side of the crayon for making wide, sweeping designs. Show them how the point of a crayon can produce dots or lines.

For variation give them chalk to test on colored paper or slate. And give them some experience with soft-point marking pens—first the wide and then the thin-line type

All of these artistic tools afford the easiest, quickest means of capturing a child's moment of enthusiasm for creating something.

Painting

Preparing for a painting session is a little more difficult, but the results are well worth the added effort. Painting presents the children the opportunity to create in a larger, broader, freer way than that which is associated with drawing materials.

After you have fortified each artist with a smock, rags, water and newspaper, introduce the brush. Show how to hold it. Let the children demonstrate some of the ways to use it so the effect is different: split, tap, twist, press, roll, mix paints, paint color on color. Let them experiment in their own ways. Then let each child tell what his painting is about—if it has a "story." Provide a clothesline, table, counter or floor space adequate for the drying of finished paintings. Make sure that the responsibility for clean-up is part of the art activity.

What To Do with Completed Paintings and Drawings

Children put a good deal of heart and mind into producing a painting or drawing. You and the other playgroup parents should save an ample selection of such lovingly executed artwork. The children feel rewarded when you show your delight by hanging their work on a refrigerator door or wall for a while. If you like a tidier way to put up artwork, a bulletin board is an easy solution. Most effective of all is the use of a large picture frame hung in a room where the family often gathers. Children's work hung inside it may be regularly changed.

When the display period is over the work may be stored for use at appropriate times as gift-wrapping. Gift tags or cards for special occasions may be made by cutting drawings or paintings with regular scissors or pinking shears. A gift box wrapped in tissue paper may be dressed up in a personal way by gluing a picture or part of a painting to the top of a box.

The day that Grandpa is sick, and you know a child-made remembrance would help to brighten his room, may not be the day when the child is in the mood to make something. Treasures saved from playgroup projects done earlier will come in handy for the time when such an occasion arises.

Storage may seem a drawback. Simply purchase two large pieces of poster cardboard from the stationer's or hobby shop if you do not have a good substitute already in the house. Use four clamp-type paperclips to hold them together. Keep artwork pressed inside. If you feel extravagant, you might invest in an artist's portfolio. It will be in use all through your child's years in elementary school.

Tearing and Cutting

Cutting is a small-muscle motor skill often difficult for three-year-olds. Let them start by tearing up old magazines and newspapers for appealing pictures. They'll love it! Encourage them to tear an enormous scrap—then a tiny one. At first this is more fun than making a definite shape. Eventually introduce scissors—the small blunt-end ones—but always allow for the same result to be accomplished by tearing. This satisfies the child who is not quite ready to master the more difficult skill.

Once the children take up scissors you'll find them determined to conquer the skill. Don't worry about what they might destroy: It's difficult even for an adult to cut anything but paper with the small, blunt-point scissors you will provide for the children. Just provide a supply of small pieces of paper so they can test their progress. Initially you may need to hold the paper for them. They may not be able to coordinate the scissors and paper. Gradually they will begin snipping many nondescript shapes in free cutting activity. Another time give them large simple shapes to cut out. Once the simple shapes have been mastered, the children will automatically undertake more difficult tasks.

Pasting

For many preschoolers the fun of paste is in spreading it everywhere. The youngsters are apt to plunge in with little concern for results, using the paste like finger-paint, then peeling the dried paste off their fingers. Delightful! When they have succeeded in covering themselves as thoroughly as their paper they are at a loss to understand why objects are sticking everywhere but on the desired spot.

Since the initial joy is in the spreading, in early pasting experiences choose activities which allow the children to enjoy smearing away. For the young three-year-olds, actually tape the paper to the table so it doesn't slip about and use thick paper that will absorb extra moisture. The paste can be colored with a little vegetable dye for eye appeal.

Q-tips, toothbrushes or paste brushes can enhance the fun of manipulating the paste.

Enlarge the pasting experience by having paste-spreading sessions which include sprinkling, dropping or placing materials onto the pasted surface. Such materials could include paper scraps, fabric, herbs, objects from nature or sparkles. The possibilities are endless.

After much practice in this kind of activity, the children will be ready to attempt gluing materials of their choice to a surface. Make sure you have chosen amply large pieces for the youngsters' first trials at this skill. Big magazine cutouts or generous snippings of fabric would be good starter materials. Allow the children to choose the items which they plan to use for their composition before they even touch the paste. Now they are ready to use fingers or brushes to smear paste on one of the pieces. Next they carefully stick it to the surface that they are decorating. The children should have many opportunities to use paste with large materials before trying to glue tiny bits. Remember—large pieces in small numbers will provide the best early experiences.

As always the ages and individual skills of your children will determine how complicated the activity can be. As a rule three-year-olds will need more time with the spreading skill mentioned first, whereas four-year-olds will soon be ready to attempt gluing individual objects.

Fastening

While pasting is the primary means children use for putting pieces together, there are other methods of fastening. Sometimes there is a more efficient or durable way of holding parts together. Other times a new means of hooking items to one another can provide an appealing change of pace. Some of the variations are tape, contact paper, brass paper-fasteners and staples.

Tape is probably the most popular with the children. They love tearing tape off the roll, and they can stick it to almost anything except wallpaper without doing harm. Sometimes little hands have trouble tearing or cutting tape. In this case it is helpful if you cut off different-sized pieces and stick them lightly along the edge of the table or around the edge of a plate or pie pan in the center of the table. The children can then easily take pieces as they need them.

Initially tape-fastening activities should involve attaching flat surfaces. One mother happened on a wonderful two-dimensional activity. Desperate for something to keep a sick child busy, she dumped in his room some masking tape, magic markers and colored oaktag scraps left over from playgroup. The results were smashing—cars and trucks, letters, rockets, etc., all a conglomerate of shapes and colors. The mother had solved the problem of entertaining her patient and deciding what to do with playgroup next time all in one fell swoop.

Tape lends itself to creative work that is not specifically fastening. It can be used as a medium for making designs on paper, forming letters on a background or framing a picture. You might just give the children tape and see what ways they can invent to use it.

Brass paper-fasteners can give children's art mobility. Here, as with tape, begin with hooking flat pieces together. With early trials do not make the children conscious of creating anything specific. Start out with a quantity of scraps in which you have made holes with the fastener, a sharp implement or a paper punch. The children will love hooking pieces together and moving the parts. Much later and more likely with four-year-olds, you can begin doing hinged figures which require designing, cutting, coloring, and fastening.

Don't forget that some children love to save pictures and make books. The simplest use for brass fasteners is securing together the pages and cover.

Contact paper is expensive but the results of projects using it are so effective that it is worth considering it for at least one trial. A piece of clear Contact, sticky side up, provides a transparent background for collages and pictures composed of all manner of materials—leaves, sequins, paper, fabric, etc. Covered with colored cellophane it is a see-through picture to hang in front of a window or lamp. Such an activity is perfect for children who find pasting pictures too messy or complicated for their liking. For economy's sake, save scraps. Small bits can be used for making attractive bookmarks or small window hangings.

The stapler is primarily for Mother's use. Small staplers which children handle easily break quickly and the larger ones are sometimes difficult to use. Yet a stapler is often clearly the best means of attaching parts of the children's project. In such cases, it is usually best for you to do the stapling for each child.

Modeling

Of all art activities modeling is perhaps the most relaxing for children . . . a great starter for new groups still getting acquainted or a calming treat for children temporarily at odds with one another. Almost immediately they become absorbed in creating. There is no beginning or end and any mistakes or (to their minds) unsuccessful attempts are quickly demolished and tried again. Actually, for many the highlight lies in destroying one creation and starting again in a new direction. The children will often talk freely as they work, and here is another chance for you to become aware of their feelings and thoughts.

The first time you use clay or play dough just leave it on a table without any accessory tools and see how the children use their hands. After they have experimented on their own, sit down with them and talk about the different ways they have found to change the shape of clay. Ask them if they can find some new ways . . . pound, twist, fold, roll around to make a ball, or work the clay back and forth to make a snake. If it seems appropriate, give other ideas. For example, you might show how an arm or head grows out of a body by squeezing the shape from the side or top of the lump of clay. Your preschoolers might enjoy playing a guessing game: each person makes an object and then gives clues to help the others determine what it is. A circle with a hole in the center might be a wheel, doughnut, lifesaver, etc.

Another time the youngsters might enjoy using rolling pins and a blunt knife to cut clay shapes. Cookie cutters work well on firm clay. Fork tongs and spoon handles make interesting imprints in flattened clay. Sometime set out toy pans and dishes and you'll be amazed at the muffins, cakes and pancakes the children produce.

Woodworking

Few things generate as much excitement in a group of preschoolers as wood scraps, a hammer and nails. You do not need to be a master carpenter to give a three-year-old a few hints about how to wield a hammer and acquire a few other basic woodworking skills. You don't even need a special workbench.

Simply choose a convenient corner somewhere in your home where you can set out a few wood pieces, a tool or two and nails. A wooden box or old table would make a dandy workbench, but your initial attempts can be made right on the floor. When you see how enthusiastically your preschoolers respond to the activity, you might want to set up a more permanent work area.

If wood scraps are not right at hand a trip to the local lumber store is in order. Many such places allow children to clean out scrap barrels free of charge or offer sacks of scraps for sale at a small charge.

While you are in the store pick up any tools you have decided to acquire. You should avoid toy tool sets for children. Most of these are flimsily made and lead to frustration. Often they are also too small. Since children handle big objects more easily than little ones, they will have the greatest success by developing a few basic skills with *real* tools. Have on hand such items as a tack hammer and small nails with big heads. As you expand woodworking skills add a short screwdriver with a large, stubby handle, a hacksaw and a C-clamp or vise to your collection. (For more detailed information on what tools work best in the hands of children see pages 17, 74, 93, 165. Specific skills such as hammering and sawing are described in individual activity instructions.)

At home gather your group in your chosen "carpenter corner" with the wood pieces and tools. The variety of wooden shapes will stir imagination and the children will set about creating their own clusters. The final product is not as important as the satisfaction of hammering a nail. For added flair, supply a few bits of wire, string or old door fixtures for use as accessories to the objects made.

As the children work, be on hand to oversee the situation. Point out simple directions for safety, and be firm about the children's using tools in the proper manner. If there is any flagrant misuse, just remove the tools, saying that only people who use them properly will be allowed to work with them. And then try the activity again later.

When you meet with an enthusiastic response to that first woodworking session, you may want to undertake some of the simple woodcrafting projects described in the activities section of this book. You will feel fully as proud as the children, as they create small puzzles, key hangers or other special objects.

Music and You

Music is an area in which parents often feel inadequate. If you don't play a musical instrument and you can't sing unwaveringly on key, then you are sure that you are totally unqualified to be involved in helping others learn anything about music. Remember that you have at least three important skills at your fingertips: you can put a record on the record player; you know a few nursery rhymes; and you can clap your hands. If you can add guitar-playing or some other talent to those three skills, consider it an extra bonus. If you don't have a record player or a few appropriate records, you can borrow the player from a friend for the day, and the desired records from the library.

Perhaps you entertain some doubts about the nursery rhymes. This book supplies you with a list of familiar ones along with a list of songs you are likely to know. Glance over these and you will be surprised at how many you recollect. The appendix will aid you in recalling words to the songs. If you worry about your singing talents, cheer up. Young children simply don't notice if you are singing off-key. Look confident and cheerful and they will think you equal anything on television. Once you begin a song there may be a child in your group who will "take the lead" and guide the melody of songs he knows, or you can use bells, records or piano in teaching new tunes.

When you lack the proper record or song to sing, your two hands provide a wonderful source of music. The children can fill in during a start and stop music game, and they can provide all sorts of sounds and rhythms. Best of all the children have the same "instrument." They will love clapping with you.

Tunes You Already Know*

NURSERY RHYMES

1. Baa Baa Black Sheep
2. Farmer in the Dell
3. Here We Go Round the Mulberry Bush (game)
4. Hickory Dickory Dock
5. Hot Cross Buns
6. Teensy Weensy Spider
7. Jack and Jill
8. Little Jack Horner
9. Little Miss Muffet
10. London Bridge is Falling Down (game)
11. Mary Had a Little Lamb
12. Old King Cole
13. Pop Goes the Weasel
14. Ring Around the Rosie (game)
15. Rock-a-Bye Baby
16. Three Blind Mice
17. Wee Willy Winkie
18. Rain Rain Go Away
19. Do You Know the Muffin Man
20. Old MacDonald Had a Farm

*See Appendix 1 for words to most of these songs

21. Humpty Dumpty
22. Twinkle Twinkle Little Star
23. See Saw Margery Daw

OTHER FAMILIAR SONGS

1. Punchinello
2. Jingle Bells
3. He's Got the Whole World in His Hands
4. Yankee Doodle
5. Down by the Station
6. I've Been Working on the Railroad
7. Do-Re-Mi
8. I See the Moon
9. Jump Down, Turn Around, Pick a Bale of Cotton
10. Skip to My Lou
11. We Wish You A Merry Christmas
12. Oh, Susanna

ROUNDS (TO SING IN UNISON)

1. Are You Sleeping (Frère Jacques)
2. Three Blind Mice
3. Row Row Row Your Boat
4. Sweetly Sings the Donkey

How To Teach a Song

A new song can be a delight if it has been chosen carefully. Most preschoolers favor nursery rhymes or other songs that are similarly catchy and uncomplicated, short and repetitive. Learning will be particularly rapid if the song ties in with an activity or experience they have shared.

Whenever it is possible present a new song through experiences which are familiar to the children. For instance: "When you are saying your prayers at night, do you often look out the window and see the moon watching you? . . . Have you thought about someone special and wondered if they were looking at the same moon?" Then you could begin to teach "I See the Moon, the Moon Sees Me."

In order to make learning a new song easy for the children, approach it in the simplest way:

1. Sing the song once or twice so the children will know how it sounds. (If it is on a record, then play it a few times.)

2. *Say* the words without the tune.

3. *Sing* the song a line at a time, letting the children sing each line after you with your help.

4. Try the whole song together.

Music and the Children

What is music in the world of a child? It is many different kinds of sounds: high and low; fast, slow; loud, soft. It is rhythmic movement. The child finds with delight that he can move with the music, imitating the sounds and rhythms and reacting to the moods. Music is also a means of expression. A child can create new songs about his daily experiences.

A first awareness of music comes from the child's everyday experiences with sound. He is conscious of the wind in the trees, a plane roaring overhead or a hammer being wielded by a workman. If you are encouraging the children to listen to the sounds around them, you are teaching something about music. An activity as simple as tapping wood, metal and glass with a stick helps them to be mindful of different kinds of sounds. Using their own voices to say something in a high squeaky way or in a deep scary tone will help them to understand something about pitch and mood.

Rhythm is in the children's own movements. It is in their hopping, jumping and running. It is the sound of a heart thudding as a child lies still after moving very fast. By letting the children move in the ways so natural to them—slowly—quickly—they will even come to know something about tempo.

Children have a natural feeling for music and love to use it as a means of expression. The three-year-old often conveys something of how he feels by singing an impromptu original song about himself as he plays. Children can reveal emotions such as happiness or anger as they move spontaneously to the sound of a record or join the group in song.

Using music to tell a story is a favorite children's activity. Children love to take the parts of different characters in a musical record. You will enjoy choosing an appealing story for them to dramatize.

The use of musical instruments provides another opportunity for self-expression. You can help the children in the construction of simple instruments so they can learn how to make many different kinds of sounds.

Like adults, children enjoy hearing music in the background. You can relate the mood of the music to different colors or the flow of melody to line-drawing—jagged, round, smooth, dotted, etc. Putting on a record while the children have a snack or eat lunch can help maintain a low-key atmosphere. Playing a merry melody for clean-up can make a game of that task.

Music Time

Music time can be a warm, happy time—a special time for the group to come together. Assemble in a small circle to sing a song; make the circle larger for musical games that require broad movement. Often, beginning in the circle will enable the children to slip into a relaxed and confident mood, setting the stage for later open, free expression on their part. Having begun in this secure way they soon begin to feel uninhibited enough to move away from the boundaries of the circle, dancing, being imaginary beasts, or whatever the moment suggests.

In helping the children enjoy music keep in mind outside sources that you can draw upon. You may have a friend who can come and play an accordion or some other instrument one morning. Would the organist of a nearby church let you visit him during practice hours? There are a number of possibilities.

See Appendix 1 to refresh your memory on the words to many musical rhymes, rounds and other favorite songs. If you have trouble recalling the melodies, remember that virtually all of the songs are easy to find on records.

Dramatic Play

When children are left to their own devices, you will often find them immersed in imaginative play. Using body movements and language—with or without toys, props or costumes—children love to be someone else. Sometimes they draw ideas from what they know of the real world; sometimes they plunge into pure fantasy. These adventures in pretending largely comprise the dramatic play experiences of the preschooler. It is after many of these extemporaneous acting-out sessions that they are ready for more formal, directed activities.

Children "pretend" about what happens inside their own homes and what happens in the outside world. They become adults, taking the role of Daddy, Mommy or some other person important in their lives. Dramatic playtime gives them the opportunity to become nurses, astronauts or garage mechanics. Or they revert to baby times to handle their fears about a visit to the doctor, a move, divorce, sibling rivalry, or to express hidden wishes.

Sometimes children lose themselves in the world of pure fantasy—a world peopled by witches, queens, cowboys and supermen. The simplest of props—a toy, a pillow, even the kitchen sink—may inspire a trip into the world of "let's pretend."

Keep in mind that some youngsters prefer to become involved in dramatic play by themselves, while others require stimulation from members of their group or from a few props. You can encourage uninhibited, unstructured dramatic play by setting the scene informally. A box of old clothes, different kinds of hats, a covered card table "play house" are all examples of things you can make available.

While pretending is instinctive with the very young, dramatic activities can become gradually more sophisticated. As the children get older it is both fun and successful to launch the group in acting out a story in a slightly more formal way. You might read a story which is simple enough for the youngsters to act out later. You might trigger their imaginations by assigning parts and suggesting they dramatize a familiar situation such as a trip to the dentist or a shopping spree. Sometimes use a narrative record so the preschoolers can act out a favorite story while listening to the recording. On another occasion follow a puppet-making project with a little performance. Let an unusually creative group of children create their own fantasy play complete with plans for who will be monster or hero and what props will be used.

In such directed dramatic play some children may be more self-conscious than others. As with music activities, let the shy child gradually become absorbed, contributing first as an audience, then "prop man," "sound expert" and finally "actor" or "actress."

Whether the dramatic activity is purely spontaneous or planned and directed by you, you will find this kind of play a particularly rich opportunity to become more familiar with the children as individuals. A child's pretending reveals so much about his knowledge, needs, strengths and emotions.

Story-telling

Story time is a favorite time for three- and four-year-olds. A hush will settle over normally rambunctious youngsters as they hang on every word of your tale. A story you tell the children can be retold by them in any one of a variety of ways—each as much fun as the first listening. Preschoolers even enjoy creating their own original poems and narratives.

Whether you are telling or reading your story, careful choice is essential. A shorter, simpler story is required for a group than for a single listener. If possible relate the piece to a recent experience of one or all of the children. For example, a baby is born to a playgroup mother or neighbor, and others enjoy hearing a story about the family's new addition. Use a story to give more meaning to an art project or science walk. Read about the coming seasons before giving your preschoolers appropriate colors to express on paper their ideas about the time of the year. A tale about a caterpillar might expand their understanding of the creatures they have found and examined outdoors.

You may enjoy simply having the group settle around you as you read a story or poem, sharing the illustrations as you go. Keep in mind, however, that there are other ways for the children to enjoy hearing someone read. You might take the group to the local library for story hour or have another member of the household lead storytime with the youngsters. There are many excellent records that come with story books. These can be borrowed from friends or the library if your own collection lacks the selection you need for your group. You might combine ideas. For example, read aloud a story of *Little Red Riding Hood,* play a recorded version and finish by having one or all of the children tell it in their own words.

Story-telling rather than story-reading is often more effective with a group of preschoolers. You will find that telling the story in your own words and with lots of eye contact is fun for you and fun for your group. If the story is a part of you the children will readily sense the humor, beauty or wonder you find in it.

A good story-teller must not depend on the memorization of words. It is not just the words, but the way they are put together that is the key to the progression of a story. You would not want to change the essential nature of the story, but certainly there will be times when you'll wish to alter it to suit different circumstances or audiences. You'll want to build a reserve of words, choosing sometimes for sound, other times for meaning.

Tell the story simply, directly and sincerely. Story-telling is a shared experience. You will communicate the anger, sorrow or joy of the tale to your listeners by the tone of your voice, some body movement, or your facial expression. No two tellings will be alike.

Sometimes you may need or want props for your story-telling. The lion hunt is a favorite one which may be enhanced by special sound effects. The presentation of nursery tales, favorite short books, story songs and poems can be nicely reinforced with a flannel board (see November activities). Puppets can also help to bring a story to life for the children.

A variety of activities add to the fun of repeating old stories and creating originals. Short sequence stories—placing three or four picture cards in order—is an idea for either freshly imagined or familiar stories. Illustrations from old magazines or nursery rhyme books can be cut up and glued to sets of cards made from shirt cardboards. Four-year-olds might even enjoy making picture cards from scratch.

If the children love to dramatize, let them first enjoy a series of very familiar tales such as those about Peter Rabbit, and then take parts of different characters. Favorites such as *Three Billy Goats Gruff*, *Millions of Cats*, and *The Bundle Book* have sufficient repetition to make them easy for the group to retell by dramatizing, with or without props such as puppets or flannel boards.

Preschoolers have lively imaginations, and creating stories comes easily for many. They might enjoy devising a continuing story, with each child adding his part where another has left off. If there are five in a group, one begins and another ends the story and the three others supply the middle. This idea can also be used in the retelling of familiar stories. If three of the children cover a whole story, let the next child begin a new one.

Books are special treats, and often the best-loved ones are those homemade. Children can make books on a variety of topics (see March activity) and add pages to them throughout the year.

Be adventurous and try a variety of approaches to story-telling and reading. You and your little group will find the experience an enriching one.

Science

Children are always full of questions about the things around them. Many of the inquiries are about nature, many are related to their experiences with the senses of smell, sight, touch, hearing and taste. If you had not planned on including these areas in your playgroup activities you will find they just naturally become part of your experience together. The children are *aware* of the seasons changing and want to know why. They *collect* caterpillars in a jar and wonder what happens to them when they let them free again. They observe that big puddles gradually disappear once the sun comes out and want to know where they have gone. They begin to understand how things grow as they *experiment* with seeds, soil, water and sunlight. They have an immense sense of satisfaction as they watch jungle marigolds which they planted indoors in late November bloom for Valentine's Day.

Nature provides the perfect background for scientific discovery. You will find the children approaching nature through their senses. They touch the dandelion and then pull it apart to see how it is made. They watch birds building a nest or sit by a pond and listen to peepers and bullfrogs. They smell pines in the woods and find pleasure in touching the different kinds of tree bark from rough pine to smooth birch. Children find great pleasure in exploring objects in detail.

Nature activities for the very young child are difficult to program in detail or rush through quickly. It is more a matter of timely exposure and letting each child ask questions about and absorb facts about things he is interested in and able to understand. Taking walks is a favorite playgroup activity and a wonderful way for preschoolers to experience and appreciate nature. Bags for collecting, a big magnifying glass and a jackknife for you to use are excellent aids for investigating. You are not limited to sunny days. A windy day with lovely moving clouds, or a dull, damp day—each has its special sights and smells. Even on a snowy winter day it is worth the challenge of boots, ski pants and mittens for a time outside. If you walk a familiar route the children will notice landmarks and the changes that come with different seasons.

Nature-oriented walks are like treasure hunts. Who can find the first new plant growth hiding under the last snow? Walk along a beach and see how many sea creatures you can capture with a pail or net. Spread a sheet out in an autumn field and come back later to see what has collected on it. Go out in a snowstorm and catch different-shaped flakes on a piece of black construction paper. The treasures collected and sights seen can become an integral part of your next art project. You will find it a relaxing time for yourself and group, and the children will delight in exploring, collecting and experimenting individually and together.

On days when outdoor activities are impossible, you can provide a number of indoor activities which involve the senses—objects of different textures to feel, foods of various tastes, things to smell. A careful selection of library books can expand on what you all saw on the sunny day when you found the caterpillar or picked leaves of changing color.

Your role is to set the stage for the outdoor or indoor activity. Plan where you will go on your special walk, or set up a simple experiment. Help the children to interpret what they are experiencing. Provide the name for something that is new to your little ones. Give a brief explanation when interest is high. Ask the children questions that lead them to new discovery. Be ready to change your objectives as a nature walk turns into an observation of the installation of sewers. You will find yourself developing a keener awareness of the things around you as you help your preschoolers.

Cooking

What child doesn't enjoy licking the frosting off the beaters or stirring a batter of sugar and spice? The special likings and ideas of a group of young children can change the culinary department from Mother's routine to sheer delight. There are many kitchen projects to do, from making creative sandwich fillings to decorating cookies, with nibbling and sampling as part of the plan. The pleasure of snacktime or lunch is increased tenfold when the goodies are made by the children themselves.

Part of the joy in cooking is sharing what you make. The children love preparing some treat, then inviting an elderly neighbor for tea. This is special fun at holidays when you want to convey the idea of thinking of others, but are not ready to plunge into a traditional activity which may overexcite the group too early.

In planning your kitchen fun, choose an activity that is short enough so the children will see the results rather promptly. You can facilitate this by doing part of the work ahead of time. Premeasure ingredients. Do several steps of a longish recipe, leaving the last part for the children to complete. For example, if you decide to give them the experience of making home-baked bread, then mix the dough and let it rise once before the children come. They can do the kneading, watch it rise and bake a small loaf to take home. Have the equipment set out. Whenever it is possible, give each child his own set of materials to use, so there is a minimum of long waits for turns.

Sometimes you will have each child do the same activity at the same time. On other occasions you may organize a joint activity such as making cranberry relish, where one person puts oranges and cranberries into a grinder, another grinds while a third child stirs in the sugar and a fourth fills the jars.

A little planning—a little work—a lot of fun. *Bon appétit* with the children!

Trips

Both three- and four-year-olds tire easily, especially when they are doing something unfamiliar in a group. This is why short trips are best: a picnic by a duck pond only five minutes away by car, a visit to a florist around the corner where you can walk for a breath of spring in midwinter, or a trip to the bakery or pet shop in your town. Some libraries have midmorning story hours for preschoolers—a special treat for your group. Avoid the spectacular all-day trip with more than one excitement, and try to plan the visit at a time that is not rushed for the florist, post office, or poultry farm.

Try not to duplicate trips you know the children will be taking in nursery school and kindergarten. Always be aware of individuals nearby who have a hobby they might enjoy sharing with small children. Film-developing, weaving, ceramics, and woodworking are all examples of hobbies children would love to watch others perform.

Most simple trips can be handled by one playgroup parent, but if you have a grandmother or neighbor who would find it a treat to join you, all the better. An extra pair of hands for dealing with the unexpected is always welcome.

The trips that you plan will add fun and variety to your program and give both the children and yourself happy experiences to remember.

Physical Exercise

Specific physical exercise activities may occupy a small percentage of your playgroup time, but they are a key to its success and are important for the total development of the children. Our ideas for this department are planned so that periods of quick, enjoyable release of energy are sandwiched between two relatively quiet activities. Sometimes the need for motion arises in the middle of a long project as the children begin to show signs of restlessness. An active game such as "Mr. Rubber Man" gives them a chance to stretch their muscles. After they have exercised they are ready to finish the quiet work, spirits much renewed.

A few minutes of very active exercise can help pace a morning and gives an opportunity for the development of large-muscle control and eye, hand and foot coordination. If the weather is good and play equipment available, the children will enjoy the freedom to exercise in their own way, pumping, climbing, and jumping. Whether you have or haven't any swings, jungle gym, or the like, the ball remains the cheapest and most versatile of all equipment. Make sure you have a big one for ease in handling. It will provide the perfect outlet for energy and muscle development.

When weather is poor, games such as a beanbag toss can be good indoor physical activity. Just aiming and throwing will give the children pleasure and at the same time will develop their eye-hand coordination. As they become more skilled at making "baskets" in some of the toss games, the children will naturally become more interested in scoring. You do not want to emphasize the competitive aspect with three- and four-year-olds. Remember this both in physical and other types of games that your group plays. There is nothing more discouraging than never being the winner. Stress the fun of trying and developing a skill. Defining the degree of success is unimportant. Plan activities so each child has a chance to excel sometimes and help the children to enjoy a wide variety of physical exercise. The important point is the fun and relaxation they experience as they exercise.

Both indoor and outdoor creative "story" games provide a wonderful means of using many muscles without focusing on competition. Let the children help you make up stories about where they might be going—hopping on stones, climbing a tree, jumping over a brook—and let everyone make the motions as you tell the story. Not a bit of equipment is required, but the variety is endless. There is plenty of opportunity for moving, and everyone has a marvelous time.

SEPTEMBER

September Contents

September Guideposts

Things You Can Collect

Each month of the year has its own special flavor. The season will automatically suggest "treasures" that you can gather outdoors to set aside for future projects. You might embark on a solitary walk or on a family outing and find time to pick up a few appealing items along the way. A walk with your own children or with your whole playgroup may present the perfect opportunity for collecting items that you can use in a special way another day or take home to use right away.

If you are a parent you already know that children are born collectors. You have probably been called upon to muster up enthusiasm for a great chunk of stone presented to you in one of your child's tender moments. It may, even now, be sitting amidst perfume bottles and framed photos atop your dresser.

You may have watched a paradise of fisherman's bait materialize in moments as a cluster of enthusiastic black-faced diggers conquered their "worm mine"—a wood-chip pile in the corner of the garden! Harness this energy to achieve your own ends. Set the children about the task of looking for materials that will lend themselves to future use indoors.

Don't forget your playgroup does not hold absolute claim to these collectables. They can be a resource for rainy-day activities. Hand some to grandpa or the babysitter to keep little hands busy.

September is one of the most ideal times for collecting. The weather still beckons you outdoors. Here are some items that you can set off to find and a few hints about what to do with them later.

SHELLS

On that last trip to the beach fill a pail or two with shells. Remember blemished shells patterned by the work of a sea worm or broken pieces shaped by shifting sand and tides can be as interesting to look at and effective to use as a perfect specimen.

Set them aside for sandcasting, decorating boxes or cans, or making Christmas ornaments.

To prevent doubtful aromas, soak the shells in a strong solution of one of the enzyme wash products for a few days. The enzymes will remove odors caused by the residue of once living organisms.

STONES

Add a few stones from the beach to your pail of shells. Look for diversity in colors, shapes and textures. Expand the collection later at a quarry, along a roadside or at a building site.

Use them for counting and size games or for hide and find.

Let the children fill tiny jars with pebbles. For variety add a few marbles, shells or sea glass. Fill with water and screw on the lid. Lovely to look at!

Have a session of painting stones with watercolor designs or crayoning funny faces onto them.

Make paper weights by gluing shells, plastic beads and other pretties onto stones. Duco cement and Elmer's are good for this.

FLOWERS

Pluck flowers to press in waxed paper or between pieces of clear contact paper. To make print designs dip pressed flowers into poster paint, lay on newspaper and place paper on top with gentle pressure to make an imprint.

Dry a few for creating little arrangements later.

Method:

Mix two parts cornmeal to one part borax. Pour a layer of the mixture in a box. Spread out the flowers after pulling off the leaves (zinnias are particularly good). Pour the rest of the mixture carefully over the flowers to cover each separate petal. Leave in the covered box at room temperature for 7-10 days.

Let your energetic preschool diggers take up your geraniums, roots and all, to "put them to bed" for winter. Place in pots to keep in the house (a corner of the cellar is fine). Forget them until spring when the children can help you set them out again where they will revive.

Give everyone a turn with real clippers to cut a sprig of impatiens or begonia. Put the cuttings in small jars of water and in a week or so the children will see roots sprouting. You may help them with the potting of the new plants later on.

LEAVES

Pick different sizes and shapes of leaves. Don't neglect the pretty lacy ones nibbled by hungry caterpillars. Press them in a book for later projects or put between a sheet of contact paper and a sheet of plain or colored cellophane to make a window hanging or bookmark. (What a pretty gift!)

PINE CONES

Send everyone scurrying for pine cones in some pine scented grove. Use the finds later for birdfeeders, wreathes, miniature trees—or add pipe cleaners to make animals like turkey placecards at Thanksgiving (see November activities).

PINE NEEDLES

Scoop up handfuls of the pine needle carpet for making the pillows described in the September activities.

ACORNS, HORSE CHESTNUTS

Acorns, chestnuts and other gifts of nature may present themselves as you scour the ground. Take some for collages or counting games.

FEATHERS

An Indian headband sporting *real* feathers is a four-year-old's prize. Not enough feathers after your hunt? Alternate with home-made paper feathers or use the feathers in that acorn and leaf collage.

COCOONS

Someone may come upon a cocoon or two. Put them in a jar or terrarium where it is moist and wait for changes.

Remember the Familiar

Sometimes in our quest for the original or the unusual, we bypass the familiar. Just because something has been done before is no reason to neglect it. What is "old hat" to you may be brand new to your little people. Even if it is not totally new to the children, you can keep in mind that children love to do over and over again anything that is fun. They take exuberant pride and pleasure in showing off what they already know.

SHOW AND TELL

So when September rolls around remember the simple things—let the children tell about their summer adventures. A teacher would tell you this is a wonderful exercise in language arts. Let them show and tell about a prized possession.

FAMILY CELEBRATIONS

Remember the warmth of a family celebrating a holiday together. September holds holy days for some. Perhaps a child can share something of Rosh Hashonah with you. Share birthdays and christenings and other special days.

THE AUTUMN SKY

This is the month of migrations and fluffy clouds in an autumn sky. Talk together about where the birds or butterflies are going and why. Lie on the ground, gaze at the heavens and find pictures in the changing clouds.

Familiar things, simple things can be the making of gentle adventures shared.

September Activities

Arts and Crafts

FUN WITH SCISSORS   ages 3 and up

Materials:
  small plastic bags—1 per child
  scissors for everyone
  paper, (colored, for variety)

Method:
  Give children paper in several colors cut to moderate size for easy
  handling and to avoid waste. Each child cuts pieces to put into his
  bag. This is simply a practice in cutting skill. Some children will fill
  their bags with nondescript clipped pieces. The more advanced
  might be encouraged to try some specific shapes like circles or
  squares. The fun is in the simple doing and having the bag of bits to
  take home.

STAR OF DAVID   ages 3 and up

Materials:
  paper—blue and white, 9"x12" sheets, 1 of each per child
  scissors
  paste and brushes

Method:
  Ahead of time: Draw large triangles on each sheet. Make sure all
  the sides of the triangle are the same length.
  With the children: Each child cuts out his two triangles and glues
  one onto the other to make a star. If your group has difficulty cutting, do it ahead for them and they can just form and glue the star.

Suggestion:
  Make a Star of David mobile. Draw three smaller triangles on one
  sheet of paper, varying them in size. Duplicate these triangles on the

second sheet of paper. Also cut a strip of heavy paper or cardboard (about 2"x7") with string put through the center for hanging and three strings of varying lengths (12" and less) tied along the bottom of the strip so that the stars can be tied to them when finished.

MIXING COLORS WITH PAINT   ages 3 and up

Materials:
    paints
    paper—9"x12"—1 per child
    paintbrushes

Method:
    Initially, choose *two* colors to work with. (Early experimentation calls for limited selection to avoid confusion.)
    Let children mix colors on their papers to discover what will happen. Talk about the names of the colors they started with and the new color being made. Try another combination another time.

Paint combinations:
    red and yellow make orange
    blue and yellow make green
    blue and red make purple
    black and white make gray
    red and white make pink
    red, yellow and blue make brown.

PINE-NEEDLE PILLOW   ages 4 and up

Sweet-smelling to sleep with!

Materials:
    small bags made of scrap material about 5"x5" which have been prestitched.
    large needles (prethreaded)
    supply of pine needles

Method:
    Children fill the bags with pine needles and baste them shut or tie to make a fragrant pillow.

Suggestions:
    1. Children could collect the pine needles on a nature walk.

2. Christmas wreathes or branches from the Christmas tree may be saved in a large trash bag. As they dry out, shake the bag and a supply of needles will drop into the bottom of the bag. This then makes an excellent January project!

SHOELACE NECKLACES   ages 3 and up

Stringing is a favorite pastime.

Materials:
    long shoelaces, yarn and tapestry needle or pipecleaners (2-3 twisted together)
    stringing material
        cereals (like Froot Loops, Cheerios, etc.)
        macaroni
        snipped colored straws
        wooden beads

Method:
    Let the children sit around a table and choose their materials to string. Let them have a choice. This is an activity they can easily leave and come back to later in the morning. There will be cereal snacking as they string.

Cooking

BOLOGNA AND CHEESE ANIMALS   ages 3 and up

Materials:
    sliced bologna
    sliced American cheese
    day-old bread
    cookie-cutters in animal or other shapes—tiny ones are special fun.

Method:
    Give each child a slice or two of the bologna, bread, and cheese. Set out cutters. Let each child cut his shapes to have for lunch.

Suggestions:
    Chop up leftover bologna and cheese with knife or blender. Let children mix it with a little mayonnaise and spread it on their bread shapes.

PEANUT-CORN CRUNCH SNACK   ages 3 and up

Materials:
    2 qts. popped corn
    1 c. salted peanuts
    1 T. butter
    1 c. molasses
    1/2 c. brown sugar
    wooden spoons and candy thermometer

Method:
    Have the children spread peanuts and popped corn in a large roast-
ing pan. You cook butter with sugar and molasses until candy thermometer reads 280°. Pour this immediately over the corn and
peanuts and stir quickly in order to coat uniformly. Then let the
children shape the mixture into small balls.

Suggestion:
    Store extra in plastic bags or tightly covered containers.

PEELING CARROTS   ages 3 and up

Children have a field day with this one. "Look, Ma, no carrot!"

Materials:
    potato peelers (see if you can borrow extras so everyone can work
      together.)
    carrots
    knife
    salt

Method:

Before passing out the materials, show everyone how carrots are peeled. When each child has his peeler and carrot, move from child to child helping each to hold the tool correctly.

When carrots are peeled, cut them into strips. Children salt and munch, carrots disappear.

Suggestion:

Cucumbers may be used too, but are harder to handle.

Dramatic Play

TUNE IN ON STATION PLAYGROUP   ages 4 and up

Use for family fun too!

Materials (optional):

Tape a dowel rod to the side of a juice can and tie string to the end of the dowel for a power line.

Method:

Let the children take turns giving news reports, using the can as a microphone. "Pete caught a toad," "Sue visited her grandmother by train." They may also do well interviewing each other concerning feelings, thoughts, facts. A weather report of the moment could close the program.

SURPRISE JAR   **ages 3 and up**

Materials:
   jar
   slips of paper with messages

Method:
   Let each child draw a piece of paper from the jar. Read the mes-
   sages for each person. Everyone does what his note tells him to do.
      You can use the Surprise Jar for different things different times.
   Some ideas: something to act out (chick coming out of an egg,
   wiggly worm, etc.), special clean-up tasks, tricks to do for Physical
   Exercise (hop 5 times, run around the yard one time), toy choices.

JACK AND JILL (FINGER GAME—AND THE NUMBER 2)   **ages 3 and up**

Verse:
   Two little blackbirds sitting on a hill
      (HANDS CLOSED, THUMBS UP)
   One named Jack, one named Jill.
      (WIGGLE ONE THUMB THEN THE OTHER THUMB)
   Fly away Jack, Fly away Jill.
      (PUT ONE THUMB BEHIND BACK, THEN OTHER
      THUMB BEHIND BACK)
   Come back Jack, come back Jill.
      (RETURN HANDS ONE AT A TIME WITH THUMBS UP)

Method:
   Sit in a circle together. Demonstrate by repeating word and
   gestures two or three times, then the children join you in doing it
   several times.

Suggestion:
   Substitute for Jack and Jill the names of children in your group.
   Preschoolers love to hear their own names.

TOY EXCHANGE   **ages 3 and up**

Have each child bring a toy to playgroup. Let the children exchange
toys for a play period.
   This has the advantage of giving the children in a new situation
something familiar to cling to. The child at whose home playgroup is
being held can more easily forget the feeling that his belongings are

being threatened as he sees toys which are new to him that he may borrow and try out.

Music

COUNT AND SING   **ages 3 and up**

Method:
　Choose a song that has numbers in it.
　　Examples:
　　　Ten Little Indians
　　　This Old Man
　　　Five People in My Family (Sesame Street)
　Count together (Example: 1-10 in *Ten Little Indians*). Sing the song together.
　(See section on "How to Teach a Song.")

FASTER-SLOWER   **ages 3 and up**

A Circle Rhythm Game

Materials:
　masking tape or string (chalk for hardtop)

Method:
　Make a circle with tape, string or chalk. Clap different rhythms:
　　1. even patterns for walking or running
　　2. uneven patterns for skipping
　The children move in rhythm—slow walk, faster walk, running, skipping and so on around the circle to whatever pattern is given them.

walk, walk, walk, walk　　= ♩ ♩ ♩ ♩ or long, long, long, long

run, run, run, run　　　　♪ ♪ ♪ ♪ or short, short, short, short
run, run, run, run　　　= ♪ ♪ ♪ ♪　short, short, short, short

ski-ip, ski-ip　　　　　　♩ ♪ ♩ ♪ or long, short　long, short
ski-ip, ski-ip　　　　　= ♩ ♪ ♩ ♪　long, short　long, short

When they have the idea, the children can take turns by clapping while the others move to the rhythm.

Physical Exercise

BALANCING BEAM   ages 3 and up

Materials:
   a long piece of wood (stud) 2x4 (or any long, narrow piece of wood
      that seems suitable for the activity).
   Special balancing beams are sold as gym equipment. If you
      already have one, fine.

Method:
   Let the children practice on the beam. Let them suggest what can be
   done on it. You can supplement their ideas:
   Be a tight rope walker; walk forward; move backward; hop over it;
   straddle it; jump off; play "follow the leader."

Variation:
   Use chalk or tape to draw a long wide line on kitchen or basement
   floor or on driveway. Use like beam.

CALL BALL   ages 4 and up

Materials:
   ball (large)

Method:
   Form a circle with one person in the center with the ball. Person in
   center tosses ball up gently and calls the name of a group member.
   The child called tries to catch the ball before it bounces more than
   once.

TRAIN GAME   ages 3 and up

Material:
   long rope or piece of string

Method:
   Children line up to make a "train." Have the rope go along one side
   of the "train," across the front and down the other side. The
   children hold the rope with each hand. Children take turns being
   engine, caboose, boxcar, coal car, oil car, flat car, etc. Being engine
   is the most fun because the engine takes the rest of the "train" with
   it.

Have the engine tell where it is going—"Through the forest," "over a bridge." The engine may be encouraged to tell the "train" to go fast down hill, to strain and pull up hill, to go medium-fast or slow.

Suggestion:
Sometimes this could be used after reading *The Little Engine That Could*. The children will enjoy "acting out" the story.

Science

COLLECTING SEEDS   ages 3 and up

Materials:
small knife (not too sharp)
small plastic bags
Some suggestions for collecting. Choose a few.

inside projects:		outside projects:	
apple	pear	*Fall*	pine seeds (under cone)
orange	lemon		apples
avocado	pine cone seeds		milkweed
acorn	grape		maple seed
cherry			flowers going to seed
		Spring	dandelions

Method:

Ask the children what seeds are for. Let them tell you what they know about planting seeds. Ask, "Where are some places you might look for seeds?" (grapefruit, melon, corn, the above-mentioned).

Inside:

Have a few items from the above list set out. Help the children slice the samples and let them pull out the seeds. Notice color differences, size differences (big avocado seed, tiny pear seed). Let everyone put seed samples in a bag to take home.

Outside:

Armed with a bag for everyone and a knife for cutting samples, look outside for examples of seeds. Use the above list for help. When your group has found a few, talk about different sizes and colors. Let everyone keep samples to take home in their bags.

Suggestion:

Supply cups with fertile soil and help each child to plant two or three seed samples. These will go home with directions to keep moist in sunny place. The first person whose seed sprouts a plant can bring it to show on another playgroup day.

EXPLORE THE NEIGHBORHOOD—WHAT'S HAPPENING   ages 3 and up

Method:

Take a walk around the immediate neighborhood.
Look for:
  road work
  construction work
  people doing jobs (milkman, postman, delivery men, people gardening, women hanging out laundry)
  special places (shops, fire station, library)
Talk about what's happening

Suggestion:

Save planned, thorough visits to the fire station, police station, etc. for a later time. This is simply a walk to become acquainted with the general surroundings.

OUR SPECIAL TREE   ages 3 and up

Method:

Together pick a nearby tree (not evergreen) to be your Special Tree for the year. See what discoveries the children make about the tree. Keep returning to the tree as the seasons pass and notice the changes.

—Let everyone have one of the leaves. What color is it? Look at its shape next to another kind of leaf. Is it a different color than the last time we looked? (Are all the leaves gone? buds on the branches?)

—Is there fruit? Are there seeds?
—Is it the tallest tree around?
—Is the bark smooth; rough?
—What is near the bottom of the trunk? Grass? Moss? Creatures?
Big roots showing?
—What is under the bark? Bugs?
—What creatures do we see in our tree? Squirrels? Birds? Cater-
pillars?

You will use only a few of these questions with your preschoolers.
Let their observations and interest be your guide as to which ones to
ask. Repeat the same questions each season to find seasonal
answers.
Help take care of the tree (remove broken branches and limbs etc.)
and its inhabitants all year. Children might put birdfeeders on the
tree in the winter.

Suggestion:
Help the children to draw their tree on brown wrapping paper,
keeping the branches bare. As they watch their tree change, they
can show the changes with cut or torn pieces of construction paper
taped on their paper tree. Start out with the large green leaves of
summer, gradually replacing these with yellow and red ones, and
then begin to strip the colors as winter comes. Some winter day they
could tear white pieces of paper snow for their branches, and then
as spring begins to appear let them add little green leaves (different
sizes and shades of green as the season progresses). As the days get
longer and warmer they can add bigger leaves. This large paper tree
could be tacked up inside a closet door.

Storytelling

SEPTEMBER STORYTELLING ABOUT SUMMER FUN   ages 4 and up

Materials:
   construction paper
   magic markers—all colors
   stapler
   items reminiscent of each child's summer

Method:

Have the children bring a few special treasures from their summer to share with the group. Talk together about what makes summer different and so much fun. Let them express their thoughts and feelings on paper with magic markers. Then write the stories they dictate. Let them do as many pages as they want. Staple all together, making a book about summer.

Comment:

Some will just draw a picture and then try to connect it somehow to their vacation. Others will think about what they did first and then try to express it on paper. Someone might even "create" a summer happening by wishful thinking. All will express thoughts that help you become acquainted with the children.

Suggestion:

Writing books is a good impromptu activity. Children's imaginations give their work variety. As they get older, encourage them to write their own thoughts.

Trips

TRIP TO A FARM   ages 3 and up

Method:

As the gardens begin to change, plan a trip to a nearby farm to watch the harvesting. Have the farmer explain how the garden and farm animals are prepared for winter. Pack a picnic snack to have at the farm.

Suggestion:

The next time playgroup comes talk about frost and gardens. Let the children help you get the garden ready for winter by bringing in geraniums, begonias and impatiens and other plants that can be kept throughout the winter.

TRIP TO SEE AN UNUSUAL PET   ages 3 and up

Perhaps you know of some one who has an unusual pet—a talking mynah bird, land hermit crabs, a tame chipmunk, raccoon babies found living in the chimney, or another something out of the ordinary.

Method:
Ask the animal's owner if he would be willing to let the playgroup visit his pet. On playgroup day go for your visit. Encourage the children to tell what they already know about the pet. Let the owner tell everything he knows about the animal—how he got it, its habits, care, etc.

Woodworking

SANDING   ages 3 and up

A woodworking skill that also teaches the concepts "rough" and "smooth."

Materials:
scraps of wood
sandpaper—various grades

Method:
Show children how to smooth rough edges with sand paper. Let them feel the rough edges before you sand; then feel the smoothness after you sand.
   Let the children experiment with sanding.

WOOD SCULPTURE   ages 4 and up

Materials:
small-to-medium size scraps of wood in interesting shapes
fast-drying glue
sandpaper
wood stain or magic markers
optional: accessory metal scraps

Method:
Spread out a good supply of wood scraps and let children select, sand and assemble their designs. Since they may need to let two pieces dry before gluing on the next, they might like to stain or color some of their sculpture parts with magic markers while waiting.

OCTOBER

October Contents

October Guideposts

Things You Can Collect

Was September so busy with back-to-school shopping and those first-of-the-season meetings that time got by without a single glorious foray into the park or woods to collect acorns, leaves and the variety of other items that you wanted to set aside for projects? October is equally ideal for gathering all the things mentioned on September's collecting list—with more to add.

THINGS FROM SEPTEMBER'S LIST

Play "how many can you find" as you send the children scurrying for acorns. Sit down together and enjoy the brisk autumn air as you count how many items each person has.

If there has not been a frost, there is still time to snip the impatiens for rooting and dig up the geraniums to save for next spring. Take time to talk about why you are doing these things. Point out that cold weather is sneaking up. ("Feel the nip in the air?" "See? Douglas had to wear his baseball jacket today.") Explain how Jack Frost is about to put the flowers to rest.

COLORED LEAVES

Now the leaves are really changing their color and leaf collection is at its best. Look to the city streets, a nearby park, your own backyard; there are samples all around you. Pick up especially pretty single leaves for the October wax-dipping activity. If you are doing your gathering on your own property, let the children try your clippers all by themselves to cut a spray or two from bushes and tree branches to take home for an arrangement.

TWIGS AND BRANCHES

Small twigs and delicate bits of branches can look like miniature trees in themselves. Have a hunt for "tiny trees." When there is one for each child, prop each into a clump of clay or small paper cup or pot

filled with dirt—and each person can create his own autumn tree by
tearing and cutting paper scrap leaves to glue or tape on the branches.
Greg's "tree" may have shed most of its leaves, so he puts on just a
leaf or two. Neil, an enthusiastic paster, may produce a tree laden
with many leaves of brilliant hue! You will be amazed at how each
creation has its own distinct personality.

SEEDS

Have you noticed that some of the squash, cucumbers and other produce from your garden are "past it"? Are you about to serve your
family the last of the season's luscious cantaloupe? Are there some
fruits on your grocer's discard pile? Are flowers going to seed? Did
you save your seeds from your jack o'lantern? Collect seeds and save
for dropping onto glue on paper for an unusual abstract design. The
more advanced could make a wonderful jack o'lantern—you draw the
outlines; children glue and drop seeds.

Try the October Pumpkin Seed roasting recipe for a culinary treat.

Remember the Familiar

Year after year October means pumpkins and costumes and trick or
treat—and year after year these all produce the same sense of excitement.

MAKING JACK O'LANTERNS

What is October without a pumpkin? A trip to a farm stand can put
everyone in the mood for Halloween. If you are lucky, maybe you
know a spot where each child can harvest his own "jack." Should each
preschooler pluck or purchase his own special little pumpkin, you are
all set for a spirited face-making session at home. Supply everyone
with magic markers for the job, or set out pieces of vegetables to be
affixed to the pumpkin with toothpicks. If your choice is one huge
pumpkin, the children can help in scooping it out and suggesting what
shape eyes or what expression you should carve.

COSTUME PARADE

If you are having the group near the time of THE BIG NIGHT, have
everyone don his costume for a costume parade. Find a willing audience—a stay-at-home neighbor, perhaps—and parade away! A
marching record can enhance the atmosphere.

TRICK-OR-TREAT BAG

A simple lunch or grocery bag can be transformed into the all-important trick-or-treat bag. Give each child orange and black crayons to make designs. Hand out sheets of orange and black paper to be snipped or torn into pieces and pasted on. You might have Halloween stickers handy to decorate the bags, or supply some precut seasonal shapes for pasting. Use these ideas in any set of combinations. By giving your imagination free rein you can come up with some of your own ideas for bedecking the bag.

CANDY OR PEANUT HUNT AND OTHER GAMES

A perennial favorite is the candy or peanut hunt. You hide the booty; they dash about, bags in tow, to discover the hiding places of the goodies.

Of course, any holiday can be an occasion to do a variation of pin-the-tail-on-the-donkey. For October it can be pin-the-hat-on-the-witch, for example.

A smashing hit at one four-year-old's Halloween birthday party was bobbing for apples—with a new twist. The preschoolers fished for them instead! Attach string to sticks and put cup hooks on the end. Screw cup hooks into apples floating in a bucket of water, then let the children take turns "fishing." Try *that* on your playgroup!

SONGS

For every season there are songs. Borrow the record of an autumn tune or a melody with words about witches and ghosts from your local library. Everyone can learn it. Test your new accomplishment on the car-pool mother or on someone from the neighborhood diaper set.

COLUMBUS DAY

The concept of someone's sailing around the world is pretty tough for a three- or four-year-old, but the exciting story of Columbus' trip told in a brief, simple way—maybe with three ships on a flannel board—can have appeal. Perhaps you can find a catchy poem or colorfully illustrated book to help you tell the tale.

October *is* full of so much to do. Choose a little of the old, a little of the new, and you are bound to have fun with your preschoolers.

October Activities

Arts and Crafts

BLOT MURAL   ages 3 and up

Materials:
  poster paint
  paintbrushes
  container with water for rinsing brushes
  paper—preferably manila about 9"x12"
  a strip of shelf paper or other large sheet about 3'–4' long

Method:
  Each child paints a picture—an abstract design in the color of his
  choice, and, while it is wet, blots it onto the mural paper, superim-
  posing or slightly overlapping the designs. You might want to help
  3-year-olds start the blotting.

Suggestion:
  If the first mural captures the children's imagination, you can do
  more. Perhaps if the group is small there will be one for each child
  to take home.

PRESERVING COLORED LEAVES BY DIPPING IN WAX   ages 4 and up

Materials:
  colored leaves (with stems for ease in handling)
  pan or coffee tin
  paraffin or light-colored candles
  water (2"–3" in the pan)
  sheet of newspaper or paper toweling

Method:
  Put water in pan. Heat on stove. Drop in wax candles or paraffin.
  When melted, let each child dip leaves in pan to coat with wax. Dry
  on paper.

Comment:
Leaves will still gradually change color, but will not wrinkle and dry out.

MAGIC PICTURES WITH CRAYON RUBBINGS   ages 4 and up

Materials:
leaves, coins, paper clips, or screening
   or
pieces of string to make spook or ghost shapes
paper clips
white or colored paper 9"x12"—2 per child
crayons—large size with paper wrapping off

Method:
Children put leaf or string on top of one sheet of paper; cover with other sheet. You clip pages together so they won't slide. Children rub the side of the crayon over whole surface of covered object. Picture will appear "like magic."

Suggestion:
This can also be used in February for Valentine's Day by placing hearts of all shapes and sizes between two sheets of paper.

PAPER PLATE MASKS   ages 3 and up

Materials:
    popsicle sticks or tongue depressors—1 per child
    paper plates—1 per child
    crayons
    paper, fabric, buttons, or other materials
    glue and brushes

Method:
    Children make faces on plates using some or all of above materials
    (strips of paper for hair, button or crayon eyes, etc.); then glue pop-
    sicle stick on bottom, so they can hold mask to face.

Note:
    Many small children don't like masks through which they can see
    or be seen. Older children may cut out eyes and nose and use string
    or large rubber bands to enable them to wear their masks.

Suggestion:
  Use for short skits any time of year.

Cooking

GRILLED HALLOWEEN BURGER   **ages 3 and up**

Materials:
  fruit knives or plastic picnic knives
  hamburgers and buns
  cheese slices cut into hamburger-size circles

Method:
  Children cut faces into cheese circles and put on top of cooked ham-
  burger. Place under the broiler for just a second.

ROASTED PUMPKIN SEEDS   **ages 3 and up**

Note: Seeds must be dried out before roasting.

Ingredients:
  2 c. dried pumpkin seeds
  2 T. melted butter
  $1/2$ tsp. Worcestershire sauce
  salt

Method:
  With children, mix seeds thoroughly with combination of butter
  and sauce. Spread on shallow pan. Sprinkle with salt. Bake 2 hours
  at 250°, stirring occasionally. Done when crisp and brown.

FROSTING COOKIES   **ages 3 and up**

A fun part of any holiday preparation!

Materials:
  baked sugar cookies in holiday shapes
  tinted confectionery frosting, small dish for each child
  individual bread-and-butter knives
  sprinkles
  Recipe ingredients: (3-5 dozen)
    1 c. sifted confectionery sugar
    $1/4$ t. salt
    $1/2$ t. vanilla or any other flavoring

1 ½ T. cream or 1 T. water (add or subtract for right spreading consistency)

Method:
Ahead of time: Mix well and divide into small, individual dishes. Tint each with a few drops of different food colorings. Fill shakers or small dishes with colored sugar sprinkles or jimmies (chocolate sprinkles).
With the children: Make sure each child has his own dish of frosting, a spreading knife and choice of sprinkles. Let children spread on frosting and decorate the cookies with sprinkles. Have them set what they have decorated onto plates of their own.

Comment:
Children tend to spread frosting generously and do lots of licking, so perhaps a double recipe would be wise.

Suggestions:
1. Perhaps at Easter children will be ready to mix, cut out and bake cookies as well as decorate them, but at first the frosting end is enough and of course the most fun.
2. Painting cookie trims instead of frosting is popular. Check paint recipe and method under Turkey Cookies activity in November.
3. If you don't feel like mixing dough use the kind in rolls in the dairy section of the supermarket—or use crackers instead.

Dramatic Play

MASKING-TAPE "ROADS" AND "ROOMS"   ages 4 and up

A kitchen floor activity

Materials:
masking tape (different colors if possible)
scissors
toy cars, trucks, etc.
dollhouse furniture

Method:
Children make tape roads or outlines of rooms on the kitchen floor. They run the cars on the "roads," put furniture in "rooms." Some may just make tape designs or try letters and words.

SHADOW SHOW   ages 3 and up

Materials:
   slide projector or lamp
   optional: background music
   light-colored wall, screen or sheet

Method:
   Turn the slide projector onto the wall or screen. At first give the
   children the freedom to experiment with body movements and
   shadows as they move between the light and the wall. Give each a
   chance to create a motion and let the others guess what he is
   doing—hammering and sawing, setting a table, etc.

Suggestions:
   1. If you have any slides taken of the group, you might enjoy showing them to complete the activity.
   2. You can also trace an outline of the child's head or body for 4-
   year-olds to fill in and make a self-portrait.

Games

BACK IN ORDER   ages 3 and up

A memory game children find appealing

Materials:
   3 or 4 interesting objects.

Method:
   Three or four objects are lined up on the floor. One child leaves and
   you or another child rearrange the order of the objects. The child
   returns and tries to put them in their original order. Play till each
   child has had a turn.

Suggestion:
   It is good to begin this with familiar objects generous in size. Start
   with just three objects and work up to more as the group seems
   ready. Sometimes it might be appropriate to choose seasonal objects to play the game with . . . pumpkin, pine bough, pussy willow
   branch, etc.

HALLOWEEN GAMES

Treasure Hunt For Witches' Brew ages 3 and up

Materials:
paper bags or pail for each child
posted list with needed ingredients pictured on the list

Method:
Post a list of ingredients that go into a witch's brew. For non-reading groups the list is a line of objects glued onto a piece of cardboard or paper. Objects can be such things as a twig, acorn, leaf, dead flower, stone, etc. Children go around trying to find these things for their own brew. The first to get them all is winner; but emphasis should be on the fun in finding them all, *not* on competition.

Pin the Nose (or Hat or Mouth, etc.) ages 3 and up
on the Jack-o'lantern

Materials:
cut-out pumpkin
magic marker
pins or tape

Method:
Cut out a large pumpkin and tack up with most features drawn in. Blindfolded children try to put nose (or any other feature cut out) on the pumpkin.

SIMON SAYS ages 3 and up

Always popular

Method:
Take the part of SIMON. Every time you say, "Simon says *(jump),*" the children follow your direction. If you give a direction without first saying, "Simon says," the children must NOT do it. If a child does, he has been "fooled."

Comment:
This game is ideal for hopping, jumping, and doing other exercises to "blow off steam" when children are restless. For children this young, do not play the version wherein a child is "out" when he is

"fooled." It is more fun for the children if they can participate through the whole game. Being "fooled" is a joke everyone can enjoy.

Music

DO WHAT I DO   ages 3 and up

Materials:
  masking tape
  piano
     or
  record and record player

Method:
  Make a big circle on the floor with masking tape (this will also work well on carpeting). The children space themselves around the circle. Play excerpts of different kinds of music . . . *When Johnny Comes Marching Home, Mexican Hat Dance,* lullabies such as *All Through The Night, Old Gray Mare* and *Pop! Goes the Weasel.* Let them create the motion that best interprets the music for them. Let each child show his idea while the others imitate it.

Suggestion:
  This activity also makes an enjoyable physical game, stressing large-muscle activity. The children can take turns saying what to do—run, hop, jump, skip or waddle like a duck or squirm like a worm—and try to guess what the others are pretending to be.

THUMBKIN   ages 3 and up

A music finger-play

Tune:
  Are you Sleeping (Frère Jacques)

Verse:
  Where is Thumbkin (both hands behind)
  Where is Thumbkin (both hands behind)
  Here I am (one hand appears with thumb up)
  Here I am (other hand appears with thumb up)
  How are you today, sir? (wiggle right thumb)
  Very well I thank you (wiggle left thumb)
  Run and hide (one hand behind back)
  Run and hide (other hand behind back)

Repeat from beginning using the forefinger for "Mr. Pointer," then proceed with middle finger for "Mr. Tallman," ring finger for "Mr. Ring Man" and little finger for "Mr. Pinky."

Suggestion:
This would be a good musical activity to combine on the same day with artistic hand prints done in paint or plaster of paris.

Physical Exercise

DUCK, DUCK, GOOSE   ages 3 and up

Old favorite. Great impromptu game for restless children.

Method:
Sit in a circle. One person is the Goose. The Goose goes around the outside of the circle tapping each person saying "duck," "duck," "duck,"—then taps someone saying "goose." The new Goose runs around the circle after the old Goose. If the new Goose does not catch the old Goose before the old Goose sits in the space left by new Goose, then the new Goose becomes "it" and begins tapping people. If the new Goose catches the old Goose then the old Goose is "it" again! Make sure that the same child is not "it" three or four times in a row.

JACK-O' LANTERN BEANBAGS AND TOSS GAME   ages 4 and up

Materials:
beanbags made by mother from orange felt in simple pumpkin shape
felt shapes in another color for making eyes, nose, mouth
glue and brushes

Method:
Children glue faces onto their beanbags. Play a toss game after-

ward—such as trying to get the beanbag into a wastebasket from a short distance away.

Science

DIFFERENT TASTES   ages 3 and up

Materials:
  salt
  sugar
  lemon juice
  unsweetened chocolate in small pieces
  utensils (spoons, containers, etc.)

Method:
  Let the children sample salty, sweet, sour and bitter. They will not categorize but instead label good or bad. Some interesting taste words may develop and they will see how tastes can vary.

Suggestions:
  With tasting, always emphasize that you do not try the unfamiliar until you've asked if it is safe. Some children are hesitant to try new things. Let them then experience the learning through the others.

SPONGE GARDEN   ages 3 and up

Materials
  Wet sponge through which string or thread has been strung for
    hanging—1 per child
  parsley seeds
  plastic wrap
  note for parents explaining care of garden

Method:
Children sprinkle parsley seeds on the sponge. Help them wrap sponges for transporting home. Hang the sponges in a sunny window and keep wet. The seeds will grow and plants will cover the sponge. Water the sponge garden with an atomizer or discarded spray bottle.

Storytelling

A SCARY HOUSE ages 4 and up

Combines art and storytelling nicely as children cut and paste to tell about something or someone.

Materials:
scissors
paste and brush
large variety of magazines
construction paper or newsprint (large size)
crayon or felt tip pen

Method:
Talk together about scary times and different things that make the children feel afraid. Give each of the children a large piece of paper. Help them to draw a large outline of a house. Ask them to cut or tear pictures from the magazines that describe what makes them feel afraid. Have them paste the pictures inside the house to make it scary for Halloween. Give each child a chance to tell about his house.

Variations: Make Seasonal
Thanksgiving: Have the children cut and paste pictures on plain paper placemats to help them express the little things in their lives they are most thankful for. Cover the placemats with clear contact paper, if available, to make them durable.

Christmas: Christmas gift catalogs are a wonderful source for this activity. Again give each child a large sheet of paper and on it outline with crayon gift boxes in different sizes and shapes. Have the children paste in gifts to fit—either ideas that tell their own secret wants from Santa or pictures of gifts that other family members might like.

Valentines Day: Give each of the children a big red heart cut from construction paper and bearing the name of one child in the group. Let them find pictures that remind them of this playgroup friend: curly blond hair; kind, sharing nature; a taste for peanut butter, etc. This is a different way to tell a friend "I like you because . . ."

St. Patrick's Day: Find the pictures of green things.

Easter: This is a good time to collect pictures that show signs of spring and to talk about the changes taking place outside.

Memorial Day: A memorial is a remembrance, so the children might look for pictures that remind them of things that they did once before. Talk about what made them think of that person or event. Don't attempt to discuss war and soldiers unless the subject arises naturally.

July 4th: Let the children hunt for pictures of celebrations: Christmas, a new baby, a pet.

Vacation time: With magic marker make a stationery box look like a suitcase. Have children cut and paste pictures of what they need to take on a vacation.

Suggestion:
Your 3-year-old group might enjoy one of these cutting-and-telling activities if you made it a group project.

Trip

VISITING A DUCK POND OR PLAYGROUND   ages 3 and up

These two ideas make a pleasant playgroup morning on one of those last golden autumn days. Choose whichever is closer or better suited to your location, or combine both if it's easily done.

Method:

   Duck Pond—Be sure the children have their own bags of bread-crumbs. Perhaps you could read *Make Way For Ducklings* ahead of time. Do they know about other kinds of ducks other than Mallards? Be sure they understand that it is not safe to tease or scare the ducks.

   Playground—It would be a good idea if you planned to have the children wear sneakers. Pack a picnic snack, making sure to include a large thermos of cider or juice.

Woodworking

Children love to experiment with tools. Have enough tools so each person can have one, if possible. Plan with the children who will hammer and who will screw, then exchange tools. Adequate space and supervision will insure safety at woodworking times.

HAMMERING   **ages 3 and up**

Materials:

   workbench, old table, packing crate or cellar floor
   lumber scraps
   large nails with big heads, 1-1 ¹/₂ '' long
   hammers
   Note: See page 17 for detailed information on equipment.

Method:

   Set out materials making sure they are arranged so there will be plenty of space between the working children. Demonstrate how to coordinate a nail and hammer, like this: "Hold the nail between your thumb and your pointer finger. See how a gentle 'tap, tap, tap' gets the nail started?"

Remind everyone that "bang, bang" begins when the nail is part way in and fingers are out of the way.

Let the children practice. Move from child to child, helping them to hold the nail correctly, seeing that they are holding the hammer so their grip is not too close to the hammer's head.

SCREWING   ages 3 and up

Materials:
lumber scraps—block-size
screws
screwdrivers

Method
Ahead of time: Nail a block or two to the bench (or on a wall stud or door frame if the children are working on the floor); then hammer nails far enough into the blocks to make holes for the screws. Remove the nails.
With the children: Show the children how to screw in a screw.

"Get the screw started with your fingers. Hold the bottom part of the screwdriver with the fingers of this hand (left) to keep it in the groove. Hold the handle with this hand (right) to turn it." Reverse instructions for left-handed children.

Let them practice with screws and screwdrivers. Give help as needed.

Comment:
This is a real problem in coordination, but we have seen two-year-olds who could not manage scissors unscrew everything from door hinges to switch plates! The thrill of working with grownup tools helps to conquer difficulties.

Suggestion:
Once introduced, these are good spare-time activities. Ability and interest will determine other projects.

NOVEMBER

November Contents

November Guideposts

Things You Can Collect

Unless you live in one of the warmer climates, November can be a dreary month. A cursory glance outdoors may leave you feeling there is nothing left worth collecting. Take heart! This is the time of the dried arrangement, holiday greens and preparations for special occasions.

MILKWEED, DRIED GRASSES, ETC.

With or without your group in tow, bundle up and set out prepared with clippers and a bucket. Wherever you look—fields, woods, the back yard and even odd strips of ground near superhighways or big cities—there are the makings for future creativity. Snip anything that has an interesting look—milkweed pods, grasses, graceful dried twigs and dozens of Nature's offerings that you won't even know the names of.

Now you are prepared for following the suggestions for assembling the dried arrangements written in the November activities art section. When the children are working remember to have them tuck in a few of the flowers you dried in September.

No one is happier than a four-year-old set loose with a spray can. You will have enthusiastic helpers who would love to aid you in gilding some dried bits to save for creating decorations at Christmas time.

If you have pieces to spare, then collage-making is forever fun. A new set of materials turns the project into a fresh challenge.

EVERGREENS AND PINE NEEDLES

Perhaps you are lucky enough to have a pine grove near you or an evergreen tree in your back yard. As the month draws to a close, you can begin collecting a variety of greens for holiday decorating. If you are able to provide precious little in the way of evergreens, use the slim supply for contact paper designs. The children can arrange pine needles and tiny bits of greenery on the sticky side of a strip of clear contact. You press colored cellophane over it, and voila! a unique Christmas card or wall hanging.

If there are evergreens in sight, but not for the cutting, you have the perfect opening for a little chat about what makes the evergreen different from deciduous trees.

MOSSES, PARTRIDGE BERRIES, ETC.

The youngsters may pause in their quest for dried grasses or pine sprigs to finger the velvety green of moss or view a partridge berry at close range. Now or later, on a special junket to a woodland area, encourage them to collect the makings for a terrarium. A few treasures gathered will reap large rewards in the creation of an arrangement that can last quite a while as a reminder of the sprightly collecting sessions you had before winter weather set in. Look for ideas on how to do it in the November science activities.

SMALL CONTAINERS

Step up your indoor collecting in preparation for the holiday season. Set aside small glass or tin containers. Ask friends with infants to remember you with a gift of empty baby food jars! The children will be whipping up candies, cookies, relish and the like in weeks to come. They will need something into which they can tuck their culinary endeavors.

OLD CHRISTMAS OR CHANUKAH CARDS

Have you saved any old Christmas or Chanukah cards? If not, one of your friends may supply you with some, or the children can find a few in their homes. In December your preschoolers can create a cut-and-paste paradise with these leftovers!

OLD CANDLES

While you are in the business of asking for last year's Christmas cards, put in a request for candle stubs. Then you can complete plans for doing November's Juice Can Candles which will make pretty gifts in December.

OLD TOYS, GAMES, BOOKS

There is a certain sense of pride in taking something old and making it look like new. Create a feeling of Santa's workshop and have the children bring old dolls, trucks, games and books they are willing to part with. Obviously at three and four they are limited, but choose the items needing least repair and help them scrub, paint and mend the toys. It would be wonderful if they could have a part in delivering them to a hospital or home. They will feel the reward of doing for others.

Remember the Familiar

THANKSGIVING

November brings the warmest of family holidays—Thanksgiving. There are dozens of ways to bring an awareness of our many blessings to your little group. Have a "Happiness is . . . " or "Love is . . . " session, Charlie Brown style. Talk about it; draw about it; cut and paste about it.

ELECTION TIME

November is election time. Vote for something—like what foods to have for lunch or what outside game to play.

FEEDING THE BIRDS

It is also time to begin to think about the creatures that have not migrated to warmer places. Discuss how the birds, squirrels or rabbits are going to take care of themselves as the snows come. Make plans for feeding the birds.

SIGNS OF WINTER

Ask the little ones what makes them know that winter is on the way. Tammy may mention that her garden is all brown and dead. Kenneth may point out his new snowsuit. Craig may bring up the fact that lots of the zoo animals are in their winter quarters now. The preschoolers will come up with all sorts of ideas with just a gentle prod from you. You might even have an appealing poem or little story handy to enhance your discussion.

NURSERY RHYMES

November days or *any* days make perfect times for the singing of a nursery rhyme or some other familiar song. Remember—your record player can lead the group if you are faint of heart.

MODELING

As bad weather sets in you will be testing your ingenuity for ways to keep the group engrossed indoors. Modeling with play dough or clay tops the list as a most successful activity and one perfect for toning down a rambunctious group of youngsters. Let the children help mix the play dough. They will love "squishing" and pummeling with their fingers and fists. One caution, however: if you want to end the day with some vestiges of your sanity, add the vegetable coloring *yourself*.

All of these "old familiars" are eternally fresh to preschoolers. You are sharing their first experiences with these ideas. Tune in; open your mind. The children are about to turn old ideas into new ones for you.

November Activities

Arts and Crafts

JUICE CAN CANDLES   ages 4 years and up

Great Gifts!

Materials:
old candles or paraffin
juice, soup, small vegetable or fruit cans
    (metal, one end removed)2—1 per child
saucepan lined with aluminum foil, or coffee tin
a nail for each can—longer than the diameter of the can
string for wick
large paper clips or medium-sized safety pins
scissors
optional:
contact paper, construction paper, children's old drawings or paint-
    ings, or any other appealing material for covering the cans
appropriate appliques or stickers
glue and brushes

Method:
Ahead of time: Prepare cans by removing label, washing, and
flattening any rough metal edges. Cut contact or other coverings to
size for fitting around outside of cans.
    Tie string to middle of nail, making sure string is longer than the
height of can. Attach clip or pin to bottom of string to weight it.
Lay nail across top of each can.
With the children: Let children help put candles into the pan and
stir over medium heat till melted. Pour melted wax into each child's
can. Allow to harden. Clip off nail.
Optional:
Before *or* after the wax-melting procedure, let children put

coverings on their cans, then decorate by gluing on appliques or other decorations.

Suggestions:

1. For safety's sake encourage children to be very orderly, taking turns to be near the stove to look, add candles, or stir.
2. If you use paintings or drawings on the outside of the can, cover the finished work with clear contact paper or spray with clear plastic (acrylic lacquer).

DRIED ARRANGEMENTS IN HOLDERS   ages 3 and up

Materials:

   conch, whelk, clam or any other shells that would make good holders

   oasis (a light foam plastic used in flower arrangements, available at florist or dime stores) or, as substitute, clay, plasticene, play dough

   dried materials—weeds, twigs, flowers, grasses (various textures and colors)

   scissors

Method:

   Child presses oasis or substitute into shell or other holder in which he inserts the natural dried materials to make an arrangement.

Variations:

   Small margarine tubs, sardine cans, pint-size wooden baskets or other containers may be used instead of shells

Suggestions:

1. Take a nature walk for the collection of dried materials or shells to use in this activity. For city dwellers, a trip to the dime store for plastic flowers or commercially dyed dried materials might take the place of the nature walk.

2. This same idea is good for Christmas, using evergreen clippings, wired cones and Christmas balls on sticks. The arrangement is particularly successful in margarine tubs.

STYROFOAM TURKEY   **ages 4 and up**

Materials:

One set per child and one set with which you may demonstrate:
   2¹/₂" styrofoam egg or ball
7 regular, multicolored pipe-cleaners (2 should match to make legs)
1 fuzzy red "bump chenille" pipe-cleaner (if not available, use a
   regular red)
scissors

Method:

Ahead of time: Twist five pipe-cleaners into loops for the tail feathers. Bind the "bump chenille" cleaner to fashion head. Shape two matching pipe-cleaners into legs and feet. Trim excess length with scissors.

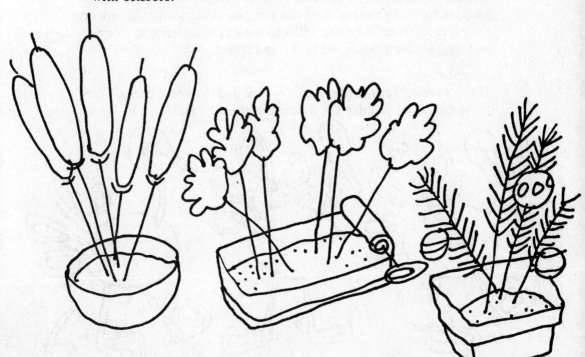

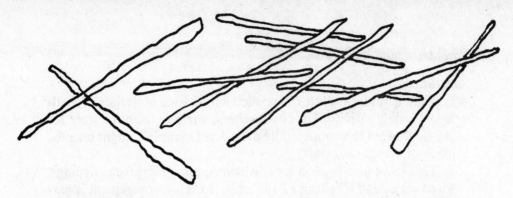

With the children: Demonstrate assembly. Stick head into narrow end of egg. Line up feathers along the back of the wide end of the egg. Stick feet in the bottom. Children then do the same thing. But you should refrain from making them place the pipe cleaners exactly as you have. The children will most likely place theirs slightly off-center, and the result will be a delightful array of turkeys dancing, running, pecking for food.

HERB AND SPICE DESIGN   ages 3 and up

Materials:
   white construction paper 9"x12"
   glue and brushes
   herbs and spices in separate shakers or dishes

Method:
   Children spread glue in small amounts in designs on the paper, then sprinkle herbs and spices over the wet glue design with shakers or their fingers. Next everyone sniffs to notice the differences in smell and appearance among the herbs and spices.

Suggestion:
   If you have an herb garden outside, pick and dry some herbs. Then let the children powder them between their fingers.

PLAY DOUGH BAKE   ages 4 and up

Materials:
  Jell-o molds
  implements for marking details:
    forks, nails
    spoon handles
    phillips head screw driver, etc.

Recipe for dough:
  4 cups flour
  1 cup salt
  1 ½ cups water
  Mix and chill

Method:
Children roll out the dough to about ¼" thick and then use cookie
cutters to make shapes. Help them transfer the shapes to a cookie
sheet. Then they use implements to imprint designs and/or decorate
with small extra pieces of dough. You punch a hole at the top if
hanging is desired. Bake at 350°. Remove from oven when shapes
are light brown at the edges. They'll resemble sugar cookies—but
don't bite in!

Suggestions:
1. Use at Christmas as a tree ornament with a frosted cookie look—or just enjoy for the fun of doing!
2. The children might like to paint the baked play dough.

Cooking

CRANBERRY RELISH   ages 3 and up

Materials:
food grinder
small baby food jars—1 per child
extra jar or dish for leftover relish
Recipe:
Put through food grinder:
1 quart cranberries
2 oranges
Add:
$1/2$ c. crushed pineapple
2 c. sugar

Method:
One or two children take turns putting cranberries and oranges into the grinder. Another child grinds. Someone else stirs in the sugar. A single child may be chosen to fill all the jars or each child may fill his own.

TURKEY COOKIES   ages 3 and up

Materials:
cookie dough (any basic sugar cookie recipe or premixed dough from grocer's dairy section)
turkey cookie cutters
paintbrushes
paint dishes
egg yolk, water and food coloring mixed to a consistency for spreading with brush—3 or 4 colors
chocolate jimmies (sprinkles)

Method:
Roll the dough, making sure it has been chilled enough to cut easily. Children cut the cookies as you transfer them to baking sheet. Let

the children paint the cookies and sprinkle them with jimmies while still moist.

Suggestion:
It might be fun to share some cookies with a neighboring shut-in or take some home to the family.

Dramatic Play

LEAF PILE JUMP-UP   ages 3 and up

Materials:
pile of leaves

Method:
The children take turns leaping into the leaves. They huddle down in the leaves, think of an animal, person or thing to be, then leap up and act it out. The others try to guess what it is. You may help by giving some ideas.

PAPER BAG PUPPETS   ages 4 and up

Materials:
brown paper lunch bags
colorful construction paper
glue and Q-tips
magic markers or crayons
yarn and trim
scotch tape

Method:
Leave the paper bag folded the way it comes. Child slips hand into the bag with his fingers over the inside fold. The bottom of the bag becomes the head. The fold will move as the child moves his fingers back and forth from fist to outstretched hand position. The moving fold will suggest a mouth.

Cut, paste and draw with the above-mentioned materials to make various characters and creatures.

Eyes can be drawn or glued to the bottom of the bag (the head). Lips or tongue may be created for the mouth area. Children might paste on yarn hair or paper hats. Someone might create a fiery dragon that shows the inside of the mouth when the fold is open.

Someone else might draw a sleeping face that "wakes up" when the fold moves up.

Suggestions:

1. Metal fasteners could also be used to make moveable eyes or other parts of the face or body.

2. Wine or liquor brown bags are narrow and would be very good for "creeping-crawling" puppets. If the bottom does not come folded like the lunch or grocery bags, you could fold it ahead of time.

3. Puppets are always popular but can lend themselves especially well to pretending, disguises and the spirit of Halloween. Puppet bags could be used for the children's trick or treat bags or if done another time of year just to carry a snack or picnic lunch or to take things home.

Games

POOR KITTY   ages 3 and up

A simple game children love and remember

Method:

One child is chosen to be the kitty. The rest of the group sits on the floor in an informal circle. The kitty crawls on all fours and sadly stops by each person to say "meow." That person must pat the kitty on the head saying "Nice kitty" without the trace of a smile. The first person to smile, laugh or giggle becomes the new kitty.

Suggestion:

There is a little bit of dramatics in this game as each child's interpretation of kitty will be different. To vary the game you may want to have a foolish kitty or one that is angry or hungry.

WHAT'S IN THE BAG   ages 3 and up

Exercising the senses—touch

Materials:

bag filled with common household items or familiar toys (bottle opener, spoon, ball, toy car, etc.)
scarf for a blindfold

Method:

Each child takes turns being blindfolded, pulling an item from the bag and guessing what it is.

Comment:

Children of this age sometimes fear the blindfold. Someone who is afraid may simply shut his eyes tight instead.

Variation:

For 4-year-olds: Children cover their eyes while one person chooses an item from the bag and describes what he is holding. "It is metal. It is smooth. We eat with it. It is not sharp." Answer: spoon. The other children guess. You may help the person who is "it" by suggesting: "Tell how it is used." "Say what shape it is," etc.

Music

MARCHING MUSIC   ages 3 and up

Listening for the beat

Materials:
record player or piano
marching music
    MacNamara's Band
    Marches by Sousa
    Anchors Aweigh
    76 Trombones
props appropriate for parades or soldiers

Method:
1. Have the children find their own pulses by placing a finger on the vein in their wrist. Talk about the idea that the pulse is a steady throbbing, beating feeling.
2. Tell the children that there is a pulse or beat in music.
3. Have the children listen to a march. Marches have beats which are grouped into twos. You will hear a heavy beat which you call *one* and a lighter beat for *two* (if you are able to use a piano you can make this more pronounced).
4. Let the children clap the beats and then have fun just marching as a parade, toy soldiers, or changing of the guard.

SAND BLOCK MUSICAL INSTRUMENTS   ages 4 and up

Materials:
woodblocks paired, approx. 4"x6"—1 pair per child
medium sandpaper unused (enough to cover all the blocks)
large stapler or glue
door pulls (if available) for handles
nails and hammer

Method:
Ahead of time: Select pairs of woodblocks and smooth over rough edges with old sand paper. Cut the new sandpaper so it just fits the top surface of each block.
With the children: Help them attach the sandpaper to the blocks of wood with either a stapler or glue. If extra door pulls are available, they may be attached to the opposite side of the block with hammer and nails. This is not necessary but gives them a special look and makes using them easier.

Suggestion:
Sand blocks are especially appropriate for train or insect sounds and as accompaniment for songs.

WATER GLASS MUSICAL—NO. 1   ages 3 and up

This shows the children high and low sounds

Materials:
a glass
a small pitcher of water
a spoon

Method:
Leave the glass empty. Tap the spoon against the glass for the note to begin *Jingle Bells.* Sing the whole song together but strike the glass each time you sing the words "jingle bells." Let each child try "playing" the glass in this manner. Talk about how they are making the same sound over and over.

Pour a little water into the glass. Tap the glass with the spoon. Ask the children what happened to the sound: "Did it go up higher?" "Did it go down lower?" Let a child pour a little more water into the glass. Let another child strike the glass. Ask again "What happened to the sound?"

Let each person have a turn at pouring and tapping. Use the song again while there is water in the glass, and have someone tap on the words "jingle bells."

Suggestion:
Remind the children to *tap,* not *whack,* the glasses or you will have a flood and broken glass instead of music!

Physical Exercise

BALL TOSS PRACTICE   ages 3 and up

Materials:
large ball

Method:
Get into a small circle with the children. Slowly pass the ball from person to person around the circle. Gradually widen the circle as the

game goes on. To make the game more exciting, you might count completed throws.

BE A RUBBER MAN   ages 3 and up

Verse:

Watch this funny, long Rubber Man,
See him stretch as far as he can.
Up go hands; down go feet.
Now relax and then repeat.

Method:

Tell the children that they are rubber men so they can stretch very far. They lie on the floor, arms up over head. They stretch, breathe deeply and then relax, as they say the above verse which you have repeated a few times.

Variation:

For bending exercises this verse is fun:

Mr. Hinges

I'm all made of hinges
And everything bends
From the top of my head
To the tip of my ends.
I've hinges in front
And hinges in back
If I didn't have hinges
I think I would crack.

Science

BABY TERRARIUM   ages 4 and up

Materials:

baby food jars or aluminum foil pans to be covered with clear
    plastic wrap
trowel
pails—1 per child
charcoal (pieces from fireplace are fine)
extra soil and pebbles

Method:
 Take a woodland walk to gather some of these:
  mosses
  lichen
  tiny low-growing plants
  pebbles
  acorns
  twigs
  etc.
 Children will pick up these items in their pails.
  At home have a good supply of soil, some charcoal and an extra
 supply of pebbles. Have the children place at the bottom of their
 containers a layer of pebbles, then charcoal, and then soil. Now
 they are ready to arrange their woodland treasures. Water and
 cover with wrap. Plants will survive indefinitely if kept moist.

BIRD NESTS   **ages 4 and up**

Materials:
 bags for any abandoned nests

Look for—
 empty nests in trees, shrubs, banks of streams, fields (bobwhite) and
  hollow stumps and trunks

Talk About:
 what kind of bird made it
 why he chose that spot
 what the bird used to build the nest
  example: string, feathers, leaves
 why you do not disturb nests still in place
  (birds may return to reuse them)

Suggestion:
 Look at pictures in a bird book to learn about different kinds of
 nests.
  You should check ahead of time to determine if and where there
 are nests and plan your walk accordingly.

MAGNETS   ages 4 and up

An Experiment

Materials:
   one or more magnets
   pieces of different types of materials:

plastic	wood	fabric	tin cans
cotton balls	small pencil	rubber band	aluminum foil
paper clips	safety pins	nail	

Method:
   1. Allow children to test one item.
   2. Ask the question, "What happens when you touch the magnet to it?"
   3. Test the other items one by one asking the same question. The children will notice that nothing happens when the magnet touches wood or fabric or rubber, but that metal objects "stick" to the

magnet or that the magnet "picks up" the paper clip. Children should leave the experiment with this idea: MAGNETS ATTRACT *SOME* METALS.

Note: aluminum or stainless steel are not magnetic.

Variations:

1. Find two boxes. Mark one YES; the other NO. Children use magnets to pick up objects. Items the magnet can pick up go in the YES box. Items that cannot be picked up go in the NO box.

2. After doing these activities, see if the children can *remember* which objects go in the YES and NO boxes. This time use the magnets to test the objects after the children have put them in the boxes where they think they belong.

Storytelling

FLANNEL BOARD STORIES   ages 3 and up

Materials:

story—short one with few characters and much repetition:
  The Little Engine That Could, Gingerbread Boy, The Three Bears)

large flannel board—about 2'x3'
  (*to make:* Cover any large piece of plywood, bulletin board, or heavy corrugated cardboard with felt and secure firmly with staples or tacks.)

pictures of the individual story characters—flannel appliques,
    drawings or cutouts
strips of felt or pieces of contact felt paper
glue

Method:
    Ahead of time: Glue felt to the backs of the story character pic-
    tures. Arrange the figures on a tray in story sequence.
    With the children: Tell one or more stories. Place the figures on
    the flannel board to illustrate the story as you talk. Prop board at a
    slant. This helps the pictures stick well.

Suggestions:
    If the children really enjoy the experience let them each have a turn
    telling one of the stories using the flannel board and figures.
    Perhaps they would like to have their own individual flannel boards.

Optional: Small flannel boards:

Materials:
    felt or flannel
        5"x6"—1 piece (to make pocket)
        10"x13"—2 pieces for each piece of cardboard
    shirt cardboard or cardboard pieces 9"x12"
    yarn and darning needle

Method:
    On the outside center of one 9"x12" flannel place pocket piece. Sew
    with running stitch to make a pocket to fit a child's hand. Sandwich
    a cardboard piece between this and the remaining large flannel
    piece. Sew together along the outer edges of the flannel pieces.
    (This avoids having to push a needle through the cardboard, which
    is slightly smaller than the flannel.)

Suggestion:
    Simplify by taping or stapling pocket to back of cardboard and
    similarly attaching large flannel piece to the front of cardboard.

Variations:
    1. *First experience*—let them just play with the material shapes on
    the board.

2. Children can make up a story about some figures that you provide.

3. Older children can cut out their own story figures.

4. Use a blackboard instead of the flannel board and draw simple figures as you or they tell the story.

Trip

GOING TO WORK WITH DADDY OR MOMMY   **ages 4 and up**

There is nothing so special as a trip to the place where Daddy or Mommy works! Does your child's daddy or mommy work in a hospital, school, lab, factory, store, or on a buildng site? Whether they work at one of these or at some other, it would be equally thrilling to see what goes on at that special place.

Dad or Mom can make arrangements ahead of time to meet the children and take them on a tour. They can give a brief simple explanation of what is made or done here. Look at Daddy's or Mommy's tools, desk, lunch room, other areas of interest.

Comment:

If Daddy's or Mommy's office is nearby and a simple operation to see, then this would also be fine for most three-year-olds to enjoy as a group. Something as vast as a hospital that requires a long trip into the city would be easier to do with a three-year-old by himself or to postpone until the group is older.

Woodworking

WOOD ON WOOD COLLAGE   ages 4 and up

Materials:
> 1 wood piece per child about ¾" thick, large enough to enable a
> child to nail on several smaller pieces (example, 12"x10")
> hammers
> wood scraps—a large supply in interesting shapes (not too small or
> they will split)
> sandpaper
> *optional:* paint or magic marker
> glue (for pieces of wood accidentally split when hammering)

Method:
> Let children launch into hammering wood scraps to the larger
> board. Some children may wish to smooth rough edges with sand-
> paper. If the smaller scraps split when nailed, produce glue to at-
> tach them.

Note:
> Wood scraps may be obtained from a lumberyard or building site.

Suggestion:
> Some children may have interest in using paint or magic marker to
> make their designs colorful. This will add to the three-dimensional
> effect and can be done during free time at playgroup or later at
> home.

DECEMBER

December Contents

December Guideposts

Things You Can Collect

December is the month that generates the highest degree of excitement. The whole time your preschoolers will remain perched on a plateau of intense enthusiasm, testing your resources and patience. Their sense of anticipation will result, at times, in swift degeneration of behavior. Fortunately there is ample to do to channel all their pent-up energy—lots to do, for lots of projects. If you pursued every possibility for what to do in the month of December you would *never* complete everything!

EVERGREENS

If you didn't have time to gather evergreens in November, wrap up everyone, toasty-warm, and go out for a clipping session. If you do not have the resources for pine boughs, your florist or nursery may be willing to donate scraps for your nursery set. On returning, the children can create small arrangements in dimestore snifters, baby food jars or margarine containers, adding tiny Christmas balls and other frills for a Christmasy look. You might have them help you decorate your house with some of the larger greens, or send everyone home with sprays as a surprise for the family.

RIBBONS AND WRAPPING SCRAPS

Maybe you are a ribbon-and-paper-saver. If you are not, turn to the other playgroup mothers or a thrifty friend. Surely there are scraps from current gift-wrapping about. Collect some of the pieces that have been hoarded and have a gift-wrapping "party." You have probably set aside JUICE CAN CANDLES or the results of some other project for your preschoolers to give as Christmas or Chanukah gifts.

LITTLE BOXES TO WRAP

Even if there are no specific presents to be dressed up, keep in mind
that children love the act of wrapping for itself alone. Assemble some
small boxes to wrap just for fun or practice. If you do not have enough
real wrapping (goodness knows, it is expensive these days!), then be
original. Newspaper, magazine pages and even paper bags are dandy
substitutes. Set the children loose with scissors, string and tape. Put
on a little Christmas music to add to the atmosphere. Some of the
tiniest "gift" packages can go home to hang on the tree.

GIFT CATALOGS

Gift catalogs hold enchantment for little children. They enjoy leafing
through them over and over. Gather some of these together. Supplied
with paper, paste and scissors, your group will become immersed in
snipping and gluing favorite pictures.

To make it an especially seasonal activity, draw or glue bows onto
big sheets of paper so that the paper suggests a gift box. Then ask the
youngsters to "fill the box" with the things they would like to give or
receive for Christmas or Chanukah.

COOKIE CUTTERS

As you look through various shops and catalogs now and through the
year, watch for interesting shapes in cookie cutters to add to your supply. You might find time to premix some dough so the children can
help cut out cookies. Special tiny cutters or new animal shapes can
add to the fun.

Remember the Familiar

DOING FOR OTHERS

The essence of this season is the thinking of and doing for others. Of
course the children *are* full of what Santa will bring and what they will
get. Look beyond that. You will see that a sense of doing for others
does pervade the atmosphere as the children perform the exciting
familiar rituals of December.

SINGING CAROLS

Learning a carol is half of the fun. The other half is singing it for someone else. Perhaps you will take your little troop to sing for a person at a nursing home or to entertain someone's grandparents.

GOODIES FROM THE KITCHEN

Take along some goodies your group has produced in the kitchen—a jar of relish, cookies, candy. Look through all the months' cooking activities for culinary gift ideas.

TREE AND HOUSE TRIMS

Old customs like "decking the halls" are the source of dozens of engaging projects. Make trims for trees. Decorate *your* tree. Create decorations for the house.

THE FIRST SNOW

If the weather cooperates, perhaps the first snowflakes will fall while you are engrossed in these seasonal pastimes. There is nothing so special as the very first snow of the year. Dash outdoors. Have everyone touch it, taste it, feel it. When it is deep enough and still unblemished, lie down and make angels. Come inside cold and breathless for a cup of cocoa and more holiday plans.

Shared in these simple, familiar ways with your starry-eyed preschoolers, this December will provide you with one of your warmest holidays ever.

December Activities

Arts and Crafts

BAKING CRYSTAL ORNAMENTS   ages 4 and up

A project with especially lovely results.

Materials:
  baking crystals (various colors available at hobby shops)
  cookie cutters in Christmas shapes (make sure they are the metal
      type that are outlines with no top or bottom)
  spoons (demitasse or baby spoons are ideal)
  baking sheets
  string tied into loops for hanging
  small dishes

Method:

Put the crystals into dishes. Have each child set a cutter onto the baking sheet. Have him spoon the colors of his choice about $\frac{1}{4}$" deep into the cutter. Set a loop of string partially into the crystals in each cutter so the string will fuse into the plastic, leaving part of a loop free for hanging. Place baking sheet into 400° oven.

The crystals gradually melt and fuse. To achieve the knobbly texture which best catches light, leave the crystals in a short time. Longer baking achieves a smooth, clear look. Check after 10-15 minutes. The finer the grain of the crystals, the more quickly the plastic melts.

Suggestions:

1. A single shape may be used as an ornament to hang in a window.
2. Several shapes may be hung as a mobile. Instead of putting string in while baking, keep a little area of crystal free so a hole is left for hanging, or use a small electric drill later.
3. Make disc shapes by sprinkling a thin, even layer of crystals into a circular cookie cutter, cake tin, or into any metal circle with some depth. Next place on tiny shells, pressed flowers, paper initials or shapes. Cover this with another even layer of crystals. This is most effective when done with clear rather than colored baking crystals.

CHRISTMAS TREE BELLS ages 4 and up

Materials:

scissors
styrofoam coffee cups
spoons (baby spoons or demitasse, especially good)
glitter—red, green, gold—in dishes
narrow gold braid or other ribbon or trim
gold string
glue and brushes

Method:

Ahead of time: The inverted coffee cup is your bell. To make bells of different sizes, trim the wide end of the cup. Invert and loop through string for hanging. Cut pieces of braid to proper length for gluing around the base of the bell.

With the children: Children brush glue around the base of the "bell." Help them put on the pieces of trim. They brush glue over

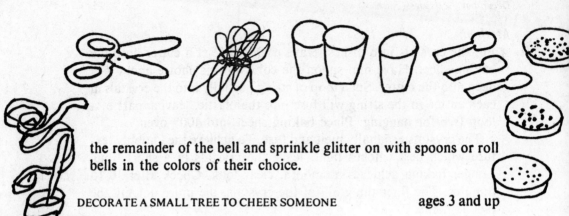

the remainder of the bell and sprinkle glitter on with spoons or roll bells in the colors of their choice.

DECORATE A SMALL TREE TO CHEER SOMEONE ages 3 and up

Materials:
    small real or artificial tree
    ornaments and hangers
    materials for making some ornaments

Examples	*Materials*
paper chains	construction paper, scissors, glue
strings of cranberries and popcorn	needle and thread, cranberries, popcorn (difficult) or Cheerios and Apple Jacks
pine cones	pine cones, glue, glitter, narrow ribbon

See also other December activities
Christmas Tree bells
Baking Crystal ornaments

Method:
Allow the children to make an ornament or two. Let them decorate the tree. With the children, deliver the tree to a shut-in person, or to a convalescent home—anywhere it will bring special cheer.

Suggestions:
1. When you deliver the tree, have the children prepared to sing a simple song such as *Silent Night* or *Jingle Bells*.
2. Jingle Bell Mitts (see page 135) could be used here.

PINE CONE ANGELS   **ages 4 and up**

Materials:
   medium-sized pine cones—1 per child
   acorns with caps,—1 per child
   milkweed pods,—1 per child
   Elmer's glue and brushes
   scissors
   knife

Method:
   Ahead of time: Make sure pine cones will stand up, stem side up.
   (Some cutting may be necessary.) Make certain acorns can be easily glued to the top of the cones, the caps making little hats on the
   acorn heads. (A small indentation may be cut into the acorns to
   help place them securely.) Split the pods and throw out the silk.
   Each side of the pod will make a wing.
   With the children: Let each child glue the parts together to make
   angels.

Suggestions:
   1. Allow for ample drying time.
   2. Ends of the pine cones may be used for hats in place of acorn
   caps.
   3. These make attractive holiday placecards.

LIGHT THE CANDLES ON THE MENORAH

ages 4 and up

Materials:
   paper menorah—cut from 9"x12" colored paper—1 per child
   oaktag or cardboard—9"x12"—1 per child
   yellow paper—quartered 9"x12" sheets
   scissors
   paste and brushes
optional:
   plastic wrap
   tape (transparent)
   string or ribbon

Method:
   Ahead of time: Cut out menorahs (cut all at one time by holding your drawing on top of several sheets of paper) and glue them to the oaktag sheets
   With the children: Give each child scissors, paste and brush, the menorah and yellow paper. Cut out a sample flame to show how. The children cut out their flames and glue them atop the candles.

optional:

You may help each child wrap the picture in plastic wrap, tape it securely, punch holes for hanging and tie on string.

Comment:

The flames cut by the children will be all sizes and shapes. Some will do only one or two flames. The creativity and interest lies in how different the pictures look—not how much alike.

If you do this at Chanukah or Passover, remember to add the two extra candles to your menorah.

WRAPPING PAPER   ages 3 and up

WITH STICKERS

Materials:

roll of white shelf lining paper—dull finish
Christmas seals or other stickers
gummed stars

Method:

Cut sheets of paper for children. They decorate them with the stickers that have been set out.

WITH VEGETABLE PRINTING

Materials:

shelf paper
poster paint
paintbrushes
vegetables (potatoes are best)
paring knife or holiday cookie cutters

Method:

Allow each child to choose a basic seasonal symbol (Star of David, Christmas tree, candy cane) which you cut in relief out of a halved vegetable with knife and cookie-cutter. Press the cookie-cutter into the flat, cut surface of the vegetable and with knife cut away outside edges. Each child brushes paint on his relief shape; then he stamps his wrapping paper.

GIFT CONTAINERS FOR COOKERY

Giving is part of the Fun of Cooking!

Materials for Decorating Containers
    colored cellophane
    clear plastic wrap
    aluminum foil
    brick paper—purchased or homemade
    paint—spray best but brush OK if paint is thick
    stickers, labels
    glue
    ribbon
    old cards or gift tags
    wrapping paper for covering boxes
    magic markers

Materials for Containers
    Jars:
    baby food jars
    small jars with screw-on covers

    Cover lids with aluminum foil or paint with brush or spray paint
    Wrap in cellophane or netting and attach small plastic spoons

    Tins:
    old canisters
    round cookie tins
    tea tins
    coffee tins with plastic covers

    Use paint or contact paper to cover up lettering on the tin

    Plastic Containers with tight-fitting covers:
    ice-cream containers (quart, half gallon)
    soft margarine tubs
    new plastic orange juice containers with tight fitting covers

    Cut contact paper designs to cover lettering on the lid

    Boxes:
    small, deep ones
    long, narrow ones

pint-size baskets that berries come in (paint or stain the old-fashioned wooden kind. If plastic, weave in ribbon on the sides)
bottom of gallon or half gallon milk carton (decorate as a chimney with brick paper and top with rim of cotton)

Fill with holiday cookies and cover with plastic wrap.

Variation: Decorate very large tins or plastic containers with lids and fill with birdseed to give relatives or neighbors.

Cooking

COMPANY FOR TEA   ages 3 and up

Materials:
Christmas cookie cutters
toast
red jelly or jam
confectionery sugar
tea set
tray and napkins

Method:
Invite an elderly person, someone who lives alone, or perhaps the playgroup driver of the day to come for morning tea with the playgroup. Have the children cut Christmas shapes from toast. In the center of each put a dab of strawberry, raspberry, or crab apple preserve. Sprinkle confectionery sugar on top like snow.

Suggestion:
This is fun and encourages the idea in a simple way that the spirit of Christmas is doing for others. Give each child a chance to pass something to the guest.

TRIM YOUR CHRISTMAS SANDWICH   ages 3 and up

Festive way for a baby sitter to feed the children.

Materials:
cookie cutters—tree, wreath, star, bell
day-old bread
sandwich fillings (any one, a variety or combination of two)
    peanut butter

   jelly
   deviled ham
   tuna
   cream cheese
small dishes filled with trims
    sliced olives   raisins
    cherries   chocolate chips
    pickles   cookie sprinkles
    dates   chopped nuts

Method:
Ahead of time: Cut the bread shapes and spread with the filling available. Put on a large platter and cover with Saran wrap in the refrigerator. Fix a small dish or paper cups for each trim. Set out paper plates and napkins for the children.
With the children: At lunchtime bring on sandwiches and trims. Let them decorate their trees, bells, wreaths and stars.

Dramatic Play

PLAYING HOUSE   **ages 3 and up**

Method:
When the children are absorbed in playing house you might find it appropriate to suggest a special dimension or direction to their play.
Examples of Ideas to Use:
   arrival of new baby
   parents leaving for a trip
   Christmas
   youngest child's birthday
   new pet
   overnight guests

Suggestion:
Supply a few extra props—baby equipment for the new baby, for example.

Comments:
Remember—supply ideas and props without imposing yourself on the children's play too forcefully. Try to choose an idea that relates to something that has happened recently to one of the children or to

everyone. For example, one of them recently may have acquired a puppy.

OR

An exciting occasion such as a birthday or holiday may be coming up. If the occasion is Christmas, you might present a small artificial tree and say "You might like to pretend that Christmas is coming to your play house and play family." Let the children take the idea from there. They may emphasize decorating, or the night before Christmas or Christmas dinner. Who knows? That is where the fun and creativity come in.

PRETENDING   ages 3 and up

Method:
  Tell the children: "Pretend you are _____."
  Examples:
    a bowl of Jell-o ("shake, shake, shake")
    a rag doll ("head and arms loose and floppy")
    a rubber band ("stretch hard and long")
    a sleeping seed in the ground ("stretch to the sun")
    a tired puppy ("yawn and stretch on your mat")
    a balloon ("get down on the floor, I'll blow you up"—when they
      are blown up, they "float" around the room.)
  They act these out with you. Perhaps they will have some good ideas of their own.

Games

NAME FINGER PLAY   ages 4 and up

Verse:
  Tommy, Tommy, Tommy, Tommy (with right pointing finger,
    touch each finger on left hand, starting with pinky)
  Whoops! Tommy (slide finger down to thumb)
  Whoops! Tommy (slide finger back)

  Repeat: using left pointing finger, touching each finger on the right hand.

DOG AND BONE   ages 3 and up

Quiet game

Method:

One child is chosen to be the dog. He sits on a chair or stool at a distance in front of the other children. The dog closes his eyes. His back is toward the other players. The dog's bone, which is an eraser, book or any article of similar size, is placed behind his chair. Choose one child who tries to sneak up to the dog and touch his bone without the dog hearing him. If the dog hears someone coming, he turns around and says "Bow-Wow!" Then the player goes back to the group and another child has a chance to outsmart the dog and touch his bone. If successful, he is the next dog.

Suggestion:

Let everyone have a chance to be on both sides of the bone. Help the child playing dog to turn and bark only when he really hears something.

Music

JINGLE BELL MITTS   ages 3 and up

A special gift from Mother

Materials:
  enough felt to cut front and back of one slightly oversized mitten
    for each child
  shapes of Christmas symbols cut from contrasting color felt to glue
    on the backs of the mitts
  two or three small bells per mitt
  thread and needle
  glue and brushes

Method:
  Ahead of time: Stitch together the mittens. With the threaded
  needle, put the yarn through the bell opening and through both
  sides of the mitt. Remove the needle and securely tie the bell. Tying
  holds better and looks better than sewing.
  With the children: Allow children to decorate backs of mitts by
  gluing on the felt decorations.
  Then:
  1. Play Christmas records and let children jingle their mitts and
  move in rhythm.
  2. Sing *Jingle Bells* together. Let children be horses prancing
  through the snow with bells on.

Suggestion:
  You may have the mitts wrapped as gifts for each child with the felt
  pieces enclosed—a special gift kit all ready for assembly!

Variation:
  Odd pairs of mittens could be used to attach bells. This is a quick
  way to make rhythm bells any time of year.

LOUD 'N' SOFT, FAST 'N' SLOW   ages 3 and up

Materials:
  The possibilities are endless. Some are:

hands (clap)	coffee tin and stick	triangle
feet (stamp)	pan lids	cymbols
voice (singing, talking)	spoons	tambourine
volume knob of the record		
player or radio		

Method:
  Sit in a circle. Try different ways of making a loud noise, then a soft
  noise. Let the children choose an "instrument" one at a time trying

loud and soft noises. If this proves of interest to them, then proceed
to fast and slow; otherwise do this on another occasion.

TAPE RECORDING CAROLS   ages 3 and up

Materials:
   tape recorder
   seasonal songs
   optional: musical instruments

Method:
   Teach a seasonal song or two. Record on tape. Play as background
   music during snack or project time—or let the children accompany
   their recording with bells and other instruments.

THE TOY SHOP DANCE   ages 3 and up

Poem:
   Did you ever see the toy shop late at night
   When all the lights are out?
   The toys wake up and start to dance
   And move themselves about.

   Dolls and trucks and motor cars
   And little wagons, too.
   Guns and drums and rocket ships
   For boys and girls like you.*

Record:
   Dance of the Sugarplum Fairy
   (or any of the dances from the Nutcracker Suite by Tchaikovsky)

Method:
   Read the poem:
   Have each child tell which toy he wants to be. It is all right if they
   all decide to be the same thing. If they all decide to be dolls they
   may be different kinds of dolls—rag doll, baby doll, china doll.
   Each type will move differently. This is true of different types of
   cars, guns, etc. Let the children talk about the toy they
   choose—how it moves, how it looks. Play the record and encourage
   the children to pretend in rhythm to the music.

   Creative Movement for the Developing Child, Claire Cherry, Fearon Publishers,
   1968.

Variation:
You might do the same movement activity with the various sections of Saint-Saens' *Carnival of the Animals*, or Moussorgsky's *Pictures at an Exhibition*. The children could move like different animals.

Physical Exercise

THE TRICK OF TOUCHING THE LINE   ages 3 and up

Large muscle coordination

Materials:
string or masking tape

Method:
You make a big circle with string or tape (tape works well even on carpeting). Everyone stands around the circle and each person takes a turn telling the group a part of the body to touch down the line.
Example:
touch your nose to the line;
touch your elbow on the line;
knees, knuckles, etc.

Comment:
Real coordination is involved while the children learn parts of the body.

TUMBLING MATTRESS   ages 3 and up

Materials:
discarded mattress or cushions

Method:
Let the children tumble as they wish. You might help them begin to learn the somersault.

Science

TREES IN WINTER   ages 3 and up

Method:
Have a walk outside (look out the window if weather is inclement). Point out an evergreen tree and a tree which has no leaves. "See those two trees? What do you notice that is different?" Children will

notice the presence and absence of green leaves. "Are they always this way?" Children may volunteer that in spring and summer all the trees have leaves. Discuss the idea that some trees keep their leaves in winter, while others shed their leaves.

Storytelling

GINGERBREAD PEOPLE   4 years and up

The smell of gingerbread ornaments baking and the delicious treat of trimming them brings to mind the favorite story of the Gingerbread Man.

Materials:
   cookie gingerbread men trimmed
      or
   cookie cutters in gingerbread shapes
      or
   children's own drawings of gingerbread men
   The Gingerbread Man story to reread

Method:
   Let the children tell the familiar story their way. Tammy's gingerbread girl may live in the city and is trying to run away from loud noises. Chrissy's gingerbread person may be running to look for a new friend. Ken and Craig's gingerbread boys may be more like the story, running away to tease or trick someone. Perhaps their gingerbread boy eats people and becomes a giant.

   How will each child's story end? Perhaps George's gingerbread people will be eaten and Tommy's will not. Encourage each child to create his own stories and not make stories alike.

Suggestion:
Milk and gingerbread cookie snacks give a party finish to this
storytime.

Trips

VISITING A NURSING HOME   **ages 4 and up**

Materials:
individual gifts for each patient—decorated baby food jars filled
    with jam, cookies or paintings the children have made
a few short nursery songs they know well enough to sing

Method:
Nursing homes can be unsettling to someone unfamiliar with care
for the elderly. It is essential that you visit the home by yourself
before planning a trip with the children. Many homes are small,
friendly places where patients are primarily ambulatory. Then it is
possible to have the patients come together in the home's living
room or reception area. This would be a more natural arrangement
from the children's standpoint and makes the visit more of a party
for the patients. Consider carefully the children in your playgroup.
You may feel they are too active to make a visit like this enjoyable.
Perhaps then you could do it with just the children in your own
family. If your group does seem adaptable to this type of situation,
check with the other mothers to see what experience, if any, each
child has had with nursing homes. If everyone feels comfortable
about their children's making such a visit and you know of an appropriate home, then go ahead with plans.
    Mention to the children in advance what they may see—older
people in bed or wheelchairs, some who are hard of hearing or have

difficulty seeing. Most children will not feel uncomfortable, and their spontaneous enthusiasm will bring joy.

GOING TO SEE A NURSERY AT HOLIDAY TIME   ages 3 and up

This is a delightful outing on a frosty morning between Thanksgiving and Christmas.

Method:
Check with the nursery to make sure it is all right for you and the children to walk around the nursery looking at the different types of trees and evergreens used in wreaths and swags. Although this is a busy season for a nursery, midweek does not tend to be as rushed and you do not really need a tour. Nurseries often play Christmas music and the children will come away filled with good spirits. Let them look at the ribbons and other artificial materials sold individually.

Suggestion:
Perhaps the children can buy a few clusters of berries or balls to mix with the cones they've collected and make a simple decoration at home.

Woodworking

NAIL BOARD   ages 3 and up

Materials:
1 wood piece per child about 9"x12", ¾" thickness, painted or stained ahead of time
nails with large heads
hammers
colored rubber bands or colored yarn or wire

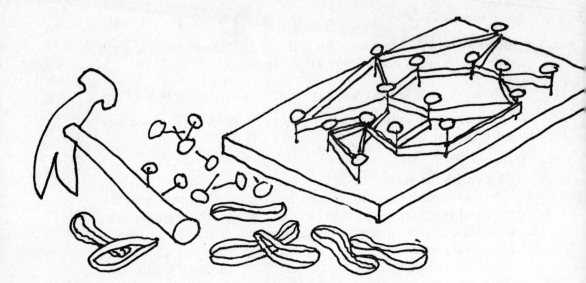

Method:

Give each child a board. Let each hammer nails partway into his board at random. Them let the children make designs—changeable ones—by stretching the colored rubber bands over the nails. Permanent designs may be made if colored yarn or wire is used instead—wrapping it in and around the nails.

Suggestion:

The rubber band nail board makes a fun game and good travel companion for long car rides or a wonderful homemade gift from a child to a friend.

Note:

Wood pieces can be precut to your specification at a lumber yard.

JANUARY

January Contents

January Guideposts

January can be a letdown after the exciting pace of the holiday season. It can also be a satisfying time. There is nothing comparable to the cozy feeling that comes when the weather is bitter outside, and you are protected and toasty inside.

Now for your collecting you will turn primarily to indoor resources. Most of your activities also will be centered inside, with the exception of a few brisk adventures in the snow.

CALENDARS AND COUNTING

Resist the temptation to toss out those last year's calendars. They will be ideal for cutting and pasting projects. To turn the activity into a game, you might suggest, "Snip out a pile of numbers . . . Now, who can find a 2 . . . 4 . . . 10?" or "Does anyone see a 5? Glue it onto your paper."

As you watch your group in action, you will notice how high each individual can count and what numbers each recognizes. Confine yourself to numbers from one to twenty. The children will have received a large measure of exposure to these numbers on television.

Perhaps your group will be content to cut and paste the numerals in their own way without any direction from you.

CARDS

With a view to Valentine's Day coming early in the next month, see if you can find any old valentines. Turn to friends who are "savers" to add to your supply. Set the collection aside for activities in February.

CONTAINERS FOR PLANTS

Nothing can give winter quite the lift that flowers can. Gather together a few containers for growing seeds and bulbs. Egg cartons are excellent for seeds, margarine containers for holding bulbs. Use your own imagination.

If you send children home with narcissus bulbs set to grow or seeds nestled in a box of dirt, remember also to send directions on care. Bulbs require the least attention; take that into consideration when you are choosing what to do.

While you are collecting containers look over the January science activity, NEW PLANTS FROM OLD. There you will find other kinds of planting activities with different types of holders required.

SNOW

Snow? For collecting? . . . If snow is falling, give everyone a piece of black construction paper. Capture snowflakes on it. Look at them under a magnifying glass.

Bring a handful of snow inside. See what happens when it melts in a dish. "Oh, dear! Look at all the dirty little bits left floating there." What a lesson in why to eat only the freshest, freshest snow! Of course, in or near a city the snow will collect debris as it falls, so it would always be suspect.

Remember the Familiar

SHOW AND TELL

The children will come to you full of tales about their holiday adventures. Let them take turns relating them. Chrissy may have brought her new magic marker. Let her demonstrate—or even share, *if* she wishes. Give everyone time to test out Tommy's new super-speed cars.

FUN IN THE SNOW

Venture into a snowstorm to run and play. There is something thrilling about dashing about amidst racing snowflakes. Riding on sleds and assembling snowmen are treats forever—as is that warm cup of cocoa when you all come inside.

OUTSIDE TOYS INSIDE

In inclement weather, outside toys can become an indoor treat. Take the sliding board into the basement. If space allows, bring a tricycle or pedal car indoors. Set up a small sandbox in the laundry room.

In one household, the success of the winter was a big sandbox assembled on the storm-windowed porch. On the nastiest days the porch afforded some protection. The children got out in the fresh air where they could burn off a little excess energy. Some sand was tracked inside, but there are few things easier to vacuum up than a little loose sand.

GAMES WITH WINTER CLOTHING

The biggest problem in taking preschoolers outside is the putting on and taking off of all that winter gear! In the interest of good sense, plan most outdoor activities when the children first arrive or just before they go home.

Turn the donning of snow clothes into a game. "Let's see who can get dressed first." Play "Who can show how. . . . ," to zip a zipper, to button the buttons, to pull on the boots (small plastic bags slipped over the shoes can aid in this task).

PLAY DOUGH AND CLAY

It is time to pull out play dough or clay again, if you have not done so lately.

FAMILIAR SONGS

It is time, too, to sing some old favorites—new to the children; familiar to you.

Winter *can* be a wondrous time—a beautiful-to-look-at, white-crystal world outside, old favorites to do and new things to learn inside. Take advantage of it before you must turn your attention to the special charms of coming spring days.

January Activities

Arts and Crafts

MAKING "LOLLIPOP" LIGHTS FOR TRAFFIC EXERCISE ages 3 and up
(See "Red and Green Light," page 158)

Materials:
> green and red construction paper, a piece of each (about 9"x12")
> for each child
> scissors
> popsicle sticks, straws or other items to use as sticks for the
> "lollipops"
> stapler; tape or glue and brushes
> pencil

Method:
> *Ahead of time:* Make the largest-sized circle possible on each
> piece of paper. An 8" pie or cake tin to trace around is a help.
> *With the children:* Children practice their cutting by cutting out
> the circles. Some children may have difficulty and will need your
> assistance. Help them all put the circles on sticks "lollipop"
> fashion.

Comment:
> This is an excellent early cutting activity because the item to be cut
> is very large and simple in shape.

Variation:
> Use any white paper for the circles and include coloring as part of
> the activity.

PINE CONE TREE ages 3 and up

A nice post-Christmas decoration

Materials:
> large pine cones, nicely shaped for trees

glue

Q-tips

small, colorful wooden birds (or any miniature birds of the type found in hobby shops, gift specialty stores, florists or gift catalogues)

optional: spray snow

Method:

Let the children glue the birds on at random. Then, if they want to spray with "snow," take them outside or in the basement and place materials on newspaper.

Suggestion:

Instead of buying a spray can of "snow," you can whip soap flakes with a little water for similiar results. Let the children spread it on their cones with their fingers or small butter knives.

SNOW PAINTING   ages 3 and up

Materials:

powdered tempera you premix in unbreakable containers to light cream consistency (3 primary colors—red, blue and yellow—are good choices)

paint brushes (large kindergarten size or small house painting ones)

Method:

Go outside. Paint on snow!

Suggestions:

Children will come up with their own ideas, but you might also suggest dribbling or spattering paint, drawing abstract shapes, making letters, or drawing simple pictures. The children may decide to experiment with one or two of the things they see you doing. Different effects will be achieved according to how wet, powdery or frozen the snow is.

Cooking

SNOW ICE CREAM   ages 3 and up

Materials:

snow

2 large mixing bowls

eggbeater
spoon
Recipe Ingredients
   1 egg, beaten
   1 c. creamy milk
   $1/2$ c. sugar
   dash of salt
   $1/2$ t. vanilla

Method:
Mix ingredients well, letting each child add one and help with the mixing. Add about half a large bowl full of clean snow. Stir well and *enjoy*.

Comment:
Perfect snack for a playgroup day with lots of new-fallen snow!

WATCHING POPCORN POP   ages 3 and up

This makes everyone feel as if they are participating in something reckless and slightly naughty!

Materials:
   popcorn popper
   oil
   popping corn
   salt
   melted butter
   paper cups
   large clean bedsheet

Method:
Spread the bedsheet out on the floor. Instruct the children to sit on the outside edge of the sheet and to remain there until they are told to get up. Put the popcorn popper in the middle of the sheet and pop the corn *without the lid*. It is exciting to see how high and far the corn really can pop!

   Retrieve the popcorn and put it in individual paper cups with a little salt and melted butter. Someone may help pass this special snacktime treat to the other children.

Important:
The popper can be *very* hot. The children *must* stay away from the popper for safety.

Suggestion:
Follow up this activity with the Popcorn Dance (January music activity) and song, or simply let everyone pretend to be popcorn for awhile—crouching and leaping—making funny popping noises.

Dramatic Play

BOX HOUSES   ages 4 and up

Materials:
large cardboard boxes (new neighbor, appliance delivery or warehouse are best sources of supply)
large and small scissors
glue and/or tape
magic markers
old wallpaper
material scraps

Method:
Ahead of time: Cut out windows and door in each box. Collect and set out materials that will help the children decorate their houses. For older children especially, material scrap curtains, Saran wrap window panes, milk-carton windowboxes and magazine cut-outs for wall pictures are but a few ideas that the material supply can suggest.
With the children: Give them plenty of time to create their own houses. Once they are finished you will find this activity leads to dramatic play.

Suggestion:
Older children might enjoy this activity on a smaller scale. Several shoeboxes together could create a ranch dollhouse. Let them decorate each box as a separate room.

Variation:
1. Use the old trick of a card table with a sheet or blanket tossed over it to make a play house.
2. Cardboard boxes can be used for tunnels, trains, planes, boats, etc. Affix a piece of clothesline or old hose and you have a gas-station pump!

Comment:

The first time you do this with three-year-olds give them the boxes as is and let them play. If they suggest decorating, fine. Otherwise leave them to simply discover all the things one cardboard box can be, and another time this play experience will help them decorate more on their own.

HANDS GAME   **ages 3 and up**

Verse:

Warm hands, warm
Do you know how?
Do you want to warm your hands?
Warm your hands now.

Method:

Repeat the verse a few times until the children can do it with you. Encourage the children to suggest different ways of warming hands and act them out.

Examples:

Wear mittens, or a muff, hold hands over the fire, sit on them, put them up your sleeves, blow on them, rub them.

SALT OR OATMEAL SANDBOX   **ages 3 and up**

A wonderful substitute for outdoor sandbox play!

Materials:

large cookie sheet with sides or jelly roll pan—1 per child
salt or oatmeal
matchbox cars (bulldozers, shovels and dump trucks especially good)
dustpan and broom

Method:

Use either the salt or oatmeal and cover the bottom of each tray with it. Give the children a good supply of the matchbox cars (you could ask them to bring some of their own from home if your supply is limited) and encourage exchange with others for variety. They will have a grand time with their trays making roads, transporting piles, and the like.

Suggestion:

This is best to do on the kitchen table or in the basement as there is bound to be some spilling. Be sure you leave time for clean-up and have everyone help sweeping up the floor.

Games

SNOWBALLS FOR SUMMER   ages 3 and up

Materials:

newly fallen snow!

Method:

Have children make snowballs. Wrap them in plastic and place in your freezer to save for cooling a bowl of summer punch or playing a target game with the children on a summer day.

FOLLOWING SNOW TRACKS   ages 3 and up

An adventure just after new-fallen snow.

Materials:

any snack wrapped in plastic bags
warm clothing

Method:

Bundle the children up well so they will stay warm and dry. Give each a bag and have them start from the same point and carefully make a path with their footprints—each heading in a different direction. Encourage them to go around trees, over sandboxes, under fences, etc. to make their path more interesting. When they find a good ending spot they bury their snack bag there in the snow, turn around and trace back their own footprints to the starting point. Now exchange trails, each child following someone else's footprints until they find the buried snack.

Suggestion:

If you find some bird or animal tracks in your yard, trail them and see where they end and why you think they stopped in that particular place . . . the bird flew off, a squirrel darted up the tree or a rabbit found a hole. Comment on various possible motives for leaving the ground—escape from an enemy, looking for food or taking food with them to store or eat, or possibly going off to join a companion.

THE SMELL-IT-WHAT-IS-IT? GAME   ages 3 and up

Using the senses

Materials:
   An assortment of food items with distinctive odors which children
   will find familiar, such as:

   peppermints   mustard   chocolate
   white bread   pepper   catsup
   cinnamon   bologna

   blindfolds for everyone

Method:
   Pass one item at a time to blindfolded children asking them to guess
   its name. If this seems too difficult, let them look over the items and
   smell them; *then* use the blindfolds and see how well they do.

Comment:
   Sometimes blindfolds frighten small children. Don't force the issue;
   let those who wish, simply cover their eyes with their hands.

Music

GUESS THE SOUND   ages 4 and up

Different kinds of sounds

Materials:
   different sizes of pots and pans
   metal Band-Aid box
   wooden or metal spoons
   any wooden objects
   different sizes of glasses or bottles (with teaspoon for striking)
   crumpled paper or foil
   tight rubber bands or string stretched over a box or container

Method:
   Collect some of the above-listed items and place them on a table.
   Let the children talk about what the items are made of. Make a

noise with each item (the children can take turns doing this).

Mention that musical instruments are made of metal, wood, string, etc. Because they are made of different materials, they sound different.

Have the children close their eyes while you make noise with one of the objects. They must guess which one you are using.

Suggestion:

Listen to records of instruments in the orchestra. Good examples are: *Tubby the Tuba* and *Peter and the Wolf*. Both have a story and a variety of participating instruments. Listen to small sections at a time for different kinds of sounds.

HIGH AND LOW SOUNDS—NO. 1   ages 3 and up

Materials:

xylophone (or a piano if you have one)

Method:

Play the scale going from low to high on the xylophone. Sing the scale using "la-la-la" or "do-re-mi". Move your hand up as your voice goes up. You and the children sing the scale as you play it. Then let each child play the scale while the others move their hands up as the sound goes up.

Do the same things going down the scale.

Now you are ready for a game. Play two notes. Let the children show with their hands whether the music went up or down. Let each child play two or three notes going up or going down the scale, followed by the others showing the up or down movement with their hands.

POPCORN DANCE   ages 3 and up

Songs:

*Popcorn in a Pot**   (Tune: *I'm a Little Teapot*)

I'm a little popcorn in a pot,
Heat me up and watch me pop,
When I get all fat and white then I'm done,
Popping corn is lots of fun.

Creative Movement for the Developing Child, Claire Cherry, Fearon Publishers 1968.

Pop, Pop, Pop, My Corn　　　(Tune: *Row, Row, Row Your Boat*)
Pop, pop, pop my corn,
Pop it big and white.
Popping, popping, popping, popping,
'til it is just right.

Tune: *Jimmy Crack Corn*
Make up your own words with the children (four-year-olds)

Method:
Let the children pretend that they are popcorn. They may jump up
and down or hop as they pretend to pop. Some may pretend to be
little kernels that refuse to pop.

Suggestions:
1. Precede the activity with a snack which includes popping and
eating popcorn.
2. Use a recording of *Pop Goes the Weasel.* Have the children
squat down on the floor. As they listen to the song they can jump up
and clap hands over their heads each time it says "Pop."

Physical Exercise

BLOCK BOWLING　　　　　　　　　　　　　　　　ages 3 and up

Good fun with a babysitter

Materials:
large cardboard blocks are best, but the standard wooden blocks
are okay

Method:
This requires an appealing combination of block building and ball
rolling. Most of the children have never bowled, so the fun of this is
letting them set up the blocks in many original patterns . . . some
may line them up while others group them or build towers to knock
down. Start rolling the ball not too far from the blocks and as the
children get better they can move farther back. Keeping score is not
necessary.

Suggestion:
Older children could have fun with this by establishing rules and
keeping score.

PENNY TOSS   ages 4 and up

Eye-hand coordination

Materials:
    masking tape, string (chalk for outdoor hardtops)
    pennies, buttons, peanuts or suitable substitute

Method:
    You make concentric circles creating a target of any desired size on
    the floor. Children are given a point outside the circle at which to
    stand. Supplied with pennies, they toss to see how close to the
    "bull's eye" they can come.

RED AND GREEN LIGHT   ages 3 and up

Materials:
    large circles of construction paper—one red, one green, attached to
       popsicle sticks or straws "lollipop" fashion

Method:
    Children line up at one side of the room, you at the other, holding
    sticks. Raise the green sign; the children move forward. Raise the
    red sign; they STOP. Whoever reaches the other side first wins, but
    this aspect should not be stressed. The real fun is that everyone may
    take a turn being Director of Traffic.

Comment:
    This game reinforces traffic safety sense, and presents an oppor-
    tunity for physical exercise.

Science

FEELING BOX   ages 3 and up

Expression through the sense of touch

Materials:
    box
    scissors
    cloth
    objects interesting to touch

Method:
  Ahead of time: Make the feeling box by cutting a hole in the top
  that is large enough for a child's hand. Line the hole with cloth and
  tape to keep the contents a secret. Put a familiar object inside the
  box.
  With the children: Each child has a turn to touch and react. Help
  them to find "feeling" words—slippery, scratchy, furry, hard,
  warm—that explain what they sense and lead them to identify the
  object.

Suggestion:
  This is a game as well as experience with language arts and sense of
  feeling. Doing a familiar activity like this each time the children
  come helps them relate to you and your house.

A TREE FOR THE BIRDS   ages 3 and up

Feeding the birds

Materials:
  discarded Christmas tree set in a bucket of sand outdoors, or a live
      tree growing in the garden
  all of or a selection from the following recipes to hang on the tree

Recipe 1: Feeding Cups
  cranberries   peanut butter and margarine
  bread crumbs   mixed in equal parts
  raisins   paper cups trimmed to a more
  birdseed   shallow depth and outfitted
  apple bits   with wire or string for hanging

  Fill cups with assorted mixtures of these ingredients.

Recipe 2: Bread Shapes
  stale bread
  cookie cutters
  wire pieces to thread through bread for hanging

  Children cut bread into shapes with cutters. String wire through
  and loop it.

Recipe 3: Peanut Butter Pine Cones
  pine cones   wire or string

peanut butter   birdseed
margarine   blunt knives

Mix 1 part peanut butter to 1 part margarine. Twist wire on cones for hanging. Each child spreads peanut butter mixture onto a cone with knife and rolls cone in birdseed.

Recipe 4: Suet Bag
suet   onion bag or other mesh covering
string   *optional:* birdseed

If desired, mix 1 or 2 parts suet to 1 of birdseed. Children help stir. Help each child wrap some suet in a piece of mesh. Put each bag on a string for hanging.

Recipe 5: Feeding Strings
Cheerios
string

Children thread Cheerios onto string. Tie ends of string together.

Method:
Follow your choice of recipes above. Hang decorations on the tree outdoors.

Suggestion:
Spread the making of several of these over two of the children's visits. Store in the freezer; then decorate the tree all at one time.

Variation:
Each child makes just one item to hang outdoors at home.

NEW PLANTS FROM OLD   ages 3 and up

Carrot, potato or sweet potato

CARROT

Materials:
carrots—1 per child
small plastic container—1 per child
pebbles
knife
water

Method:

Help children cut off leaves. Then cut off 1 inch piece from thickened end of carrot. Children put the 1 inch piece in container thick end down and sprinkle in pebbles to hold it in place.

Send home with directions to add water about half way up the side of the carrot and keep in sunny place.

POTATO

Materials:

soil

spoons

plastic cup or flowerpot (hole in bottom for drainage)

potato

knife

Method:

Cut potato into pieces so each part has some eyes. The eyes are the buds of the plant. Children spoon soil into containers and each plants his piece.

Send home with directions to keep in sunny place and water daily.

SWEET POTATO

Materials:
   sweet potato (fresh—some are heat dried before marketing)—1 per
      child
   knife
   toothpicks
   tall jar—1 per child
   water

Method:
   Help children cut off pointed end. Children put toothpicks in opposite sides and hang in jar pointed end up.
   Send home with directions to keep in sunny place with water covering half of the potato.

Storytelling

NAME BOOKS—to keep for always   ages 4 and up

Materials:
   shirt cardboards cut in halves or fourths
   clear contact paper
   small notebook rings
   shoelaces to tie
   magazines or precut pictures covering letters of the alphabet (pic-
      ture of a cat for C, dog for D, etc.)
   sandpaper, fabric or felt contact paper
   glue
   punch

Method:
   Ahead of time: Cut the shirt cardboard to size and make a pile for
   each child to equal the number of letters in his or her first name.
   Carefully cut out of sandpaper or the felt contact paper the letters
   (capital) each child will need. It might be wise to have some pictures
   precut and provide a good supply of magazines (Christmas gift
   catalogs are excellent).
   With the children: They will first attach a letter to each page.
   (Make sure the pages are in correct spelling order. Then let them

cut and paste pictures—some will do many while others just choose one page. When finished you can help them cover the pictures (not the letter) with clear contact paper, punch holes at the edge and assemble.

Suggestions:

1. Encourage the children to run their fingers over the letters of their name. They are eager to master writing their own name and this will help.

2. One sister had the idea to make a name book for her brother's second birthday. They make wonderful gifts!

Trip

TRIP TO A CAR WASH ages 3 and up

Let young imaginations make this into a fantasy trip!

Method:
Check to make sure the car wash you plan to visit is operating. Talk about how many have been to one before and what their reaction was as they sat inside the car and watched the brushes and sprays work. (To some this may have been very frightening. Perhaps then it would be unwise to go. Or if you do go, you'd want to watch the process from outside the car.) What does riding through a car wash make you think about? The children may come up with ideas such as a jungle in a rain storm or a trip through outer space. Choose the one idea they seem to like best and take along any pretend props that will add to the fun and reality of their imaginary trip—rain hats and guns for the jungle or space gear for the planet ride.

Comment:
This trip can be spur of the moment when the car needs washing and the playgroup has been more confined to inside activities because of weather.

Woodworking

SAWING ages 3 and up

If the children have had a little experience with hammering and screwing before embarking on sawing, everyone can find a woodworking job to do while awaiting a turn at the saw.

Materials:
    hacksaw
    vise or C-clamp attached to workbench or table
    wood pieces—balsa is excellent for first tries at sawing, but expen-
        sive
            or
    soft pine—in fairly thin narrow pieces (½" thick, 2" wide)—scraps
        of molding are excellent

Method:
Show the children how to put a piece of wood in the vise. Let each
child try it. Demonstrate how to hold the saw and saw some wood.
You saw, chanting rhythmically, "Slow and easy. Slow and easy!"
in time with your sawing. Let each child try holding the saw and
sawing your piece of wood briefly. Use the little chant. Now
everyone is ready for his turn with the vise, saw, and his own piece
of wood.

Suggestions:
1. Help the children to understand that tools are not toys. If there
is some flagrant misuse of a tool, put the tools away. When your
bring them out again remind everyone that tools may be kept out
and used *as long as they are used properly*.
2. Unless you are using very soft wood, like balsa, or very thin
strips of wood, the going is slow, so do not expect the children to
saw more than an inch or two. It is the experience that is important.
3. Let each child take home a piece of wood that he has worked on.

FEBRUARY

February Contents

February Guideposts

Things You Can Collect

Many of the items you collected and projects you did in the month of January will lend themselves equally well to February. In addition, you may need to plan a trip out to pick up the special materials necessary if you have chosen to do some projects from the February activity section.

LACE AND OLD JEWELRY

Rummage around for pretty frippery that will make appropriate trims on valentines—lace, bits of old costume jewelry, ribbons and doilies.

HEART SHAPED CUTTERS

Dig out your heartshaped cookie-cutters. Different-sized ones multiply the fun, so borrow or add to your own supply.

If the thought of more cookie-baking leaves you quivering, have the children use the cutters for a play dough project. Your preschoolers might enjoy cutting out hearts and pressing "jewels" into them. This is where your cast-off bracelets and earrings will come in handy. Let the result dry and present it as a unique valentine.

STRAY ENVELOPES

It would be practical to collect stray envelopes. When the children are making cards you can precut colored paper to fit the envelopes. The youngsters do the decorating. Now cards and envelopes go together.

PLANTS AS VALENTINE GIFTS

Early in February you might take clippings from your indoor plants. Impatiens and begonia are especially fast at rooting. Root them in water, and they will be all set for the children to put in containers full of potting soil and take home as gifts.

Remember the Familiar

MAKING VALENTINES

There are cards to be made for everyone—parents, grandparents, neighbors, friends. Prolific members of your group may turn out several cards, while someone else may labor over a single one or even lack enthusiasm for the whole procedure. That's okay too!

GIVING GIFTS

Valentine's Day is a time for gifts. Look through all the months' activities for a variety of ideas for gifts to make.

VALENTINE BOX AND PARTY

February, too, can be a party time. With or without the children's help you can go creative with valentine cupcakes, heart-shaped Jell-o molds and sandwiches cut out with your heart-shaped cookie cutters.

Perhaps the children could adorn paper placemats with valentine stickers or precut shapes to be pasted on—a good trick for any holiday party! They can also be set to work decorating a box for their valentine cards—individual shoebox ones to use at home or one to use at your house. For a big single one, let each person embellish one side in any medium of your choice. Of course, you will pre-arrange with mothers for the children to bring cards for exchanging.

PATRIOTIC DAYS

Remember those patriotic days—ideal for having some special marching activities. Who would like to carry the flag? Everyone! Take turns leading the march, flag in hand.

POETRY, STORIES AND MUSIC

You will not want to neglect poetry, stories and records that might be suitable for the month. You might turn to your local librarian for a few samples of what to use for the nursery set.

Winter will fly by as an especially exciting season when you become involved in using even a few of these ideas for your playgroup or family fun. If you are not too caught up in the activities, steal a moment to take a snapshot or two. Surprise the other mothers with them and use them to help you look back on these days with special fondness. Why not make duplicates of the best ones to share with all the children's families!

February Activities

Arts and Crafts

CUTTING SNOWFLAKES   ages 3 and up

Materials:
   white paper on which you have drawn (or precut) circles
   scissors
   Note: for young children make circles large, easy to cut

Method:
   Children cut out circles. Fold in half twice.
   Snip pieces from edges. Unfold.

Suggestion:
   1. Take to a shut-in person and tape on door or window.
   2. Squares may be used instead of circles.

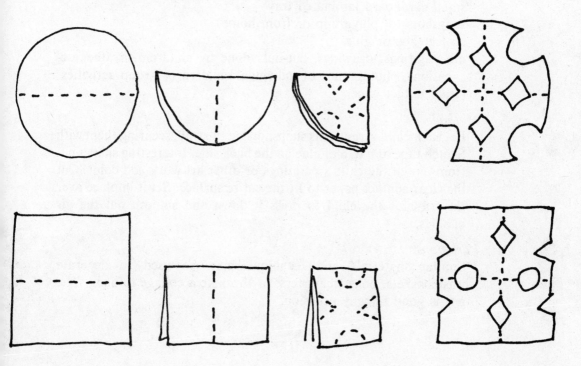

PUNCHING HOLES AND SEWING   ages 3 and up

Forerunner of following numbered dots to make pictures

Materials:
    paper punch
    oaktag or cardboard (posterboard)—one 9"x12" piece per child
    long shoelaces—1 lace per child

Method:
    Children punch a number of holes; then "sew" from hole to hole
    with shoelace.
        You may unlace the cards and let the children exchange them.

Variations:
    1. Draw from hole to hole with crayons.
    2. Ahead of time, punch their first names on the cards. Children
    draw from dot to dot to make their names.

VALENTINE MEMORIES TRAY   ages 3 and up

Materials:
    small cardboard laminated tray
    snapshots (of playgroup or from home)
    scotch tape or glue
    old paintings, drawings, cut-outs done by children on other oc-
        casions, photographs of individual children or group activities
    clear contact paper

Method:
    Let each child arrange his snapshots on the tray, securing them with
    Scotch tape or a dab of glue on the back side. Interesting shapes cut
    from one of the child's paintings or other art work add color. Cut
    the clear contact paper to fit the entire surface. Set it in place over
    the tray for the child to press it down and smooth out the air
    bubbles.

Variations:
    Similar materials and technique may be used to decorate
    wastebaskets, boxes, canisters, or to make a collage to hang. The
    gift is good for any occasion.

WHIPPING SNOW   **ages 3 and up**

The beating is half the fun!

Materials:
Ivory flakes
eggbeater
mixing bowl
water
dark-colored construction paper
paper cups

Method:
Pour just a small amount of water into the Ivory flakes and beat. Add just the amount of flakes or water until the consistency is thick (approx. $1/2$ cup water to 1 cup flakes). Give the children paper cups of whipped "snow" and let them draw with their fingers on the paper.

Suggestion:
If the snow is thick enough the children might enjoy shaping it like clay into simple snow sculptures.

Cooking

CREATIVE CRESCENT ROLLS   **ages 3 and up**

Materials:
2 tubes of crescent rolls (Each tube contains eight rolls. If there are only four in the group and no company is expected, one tube is enough.)
cinnamon sugar, raisins, cherries and nuts
cookie sheets

Method:
Ahead of time: Separate the dough and unroll onto the cookie sheets. Set out small dishes of the ingredients, chopping the cherries and nuts. Cinnamon sugar in the small jars with sprinkle tops is best.
With the children: Let them sprinkle the desired ingredients on the dough pieces and then overlap and reroll to bake according to package directions.

Suggestion:
1. The children will discover that they cannot put too much filling in if they want the sweets to stay inside for the baking. Brown sugar is a nice substitute for cinnamon sugar. Perhaps the children would like to invite a neighbor over to enjoy their special treat.
2. Crescent rolls can be used to make a quick and popular lunch. Let the children wrap the dough around a hotdog that they have slit and filled with cheese strips. This is one version of Pigs in a Blanket.

GINGER COOKIE PUZZLE FACES   ages 4 and up

Materials:
   circular ginger cookies cut horizontally into 3 equal pieces before baking
   frosting put on by you to make different types of eyes in one section, different kinds of noses in another section, and frowns, laughs, teeth, etc., in yet another. (Tube frosting would be the easiest, especially for letters mentioned below.)

Method:

Mix up the cookie pieces. Children put parts together to make their own special faces.

Variations:

1. Children put faces on unbaked cut pieces with cut-up licorice, gumdrops, raisins, nuts, chocolate bits, etc. They trade pieces after baking to make surprise combination faces.

2. Older brothers and sisters put letters on vertically cut pieces and mix pieces to make words. Frost cookies with three-letter words, one letter on each piece of cookie.

3. Use other materials for puzzle faces: paper circles on which children draw faces (cut identically into 3 or 4 pieces to make new faces); or play dough circles cut by children with cookie cutter or inverted cups (children draw faces with pencil point or stick or fashion from play dough in contrasting colors).

Dramatic Play

HIKE IN THE HOUSE   ages 3 and up

Materials:

lunch bag containing picnic lunch for each child

Method:

The children go for a "hike" through the house pretending that they are outside. Example: up the side of a mountain (up the steps), past a forest (the dining room chairs), etc. Help children decide on a good spot for their picnic (by Daddy's workbench? in a bedroom?) Everyone sits in a circle to eat. After lunch everyone cleans up scraps and papers, stuffs them into his bag, and hikes to a trash barrel for disposal. Promote some discussion of how a good camper leaves the site the way he found it and doesn't pollute picnic areas by leaving trash.

PHONE FUN   ages 3 and up

Materials:

soup cans attached to either end of a long string, 2 toy phones, or discarded older-model real phone

Method:

Conversations—Let the children show how they answer the telephone. Guide the activity by encouraging them to use such words as: "Hello," "Who's calling," "Just a minute please." (*Optional:* tape record and replay their conversations.)

Emergencies—Ask the children how the phone can help them in an emergency. "Whom can you dial?" Let each child show how to dial "0"—the operator—and practice telling a problem, the family name and address on the phone.

POPSICLE STICK PUPPETS   ages 3 and up

Useful way to enjoy valentine cards

Materials:

valentine cards (inexpensive kit variety best)
popsicle sticks
masking tape, heavy-duty stapler or glue

Method:

Let the children choose their own cards and attach them to the sticks. The stapler would be the most secure way of fastening, but the tape or glue would be easiest for them to do independently.

Comment:

Some children might think about a story and look for certain characters among the cards. Three-year-olds will just play individually with their sticks, unaware of any performance they may be giving. Older children may create a puppet show for one or two of their new puppets.

Suggestions:

1. Encourage a little puppet show only if the idea seems to come naturally from the group. You do not need an elaborate stage. Working the puppets from behind a sofa or table is satisfactory.
2. If the children are interested in giving a performance, let each child give his own show with one or two puppets. Later the children may work in pairs. Still later the whole group can work on one simple story or familiar nursery rhyme. You could assign parts and have the group act it out.

Games

COUNTING TO FIVE GAME   **ages 3 and up**

Verse:

Here is a beehive; Where are the bees? (make a fist)
Hidden away where nobody sees.
Soon they come, creeping out of the hive.
One, two, three, four, five. (release five fingers at a time)

Method:

Repeat the verse with the gestures two or three times alone, then repeat them with the children a few times.

FISHING WITH MAGNETS   **ages 3 and up**

Materials:

sticks (pencils will do)
string
magnet
paper or cardboard
scissors
paper clips
bucket or other handy container

Method:

Ahead of time: Make one or more "fishing rods" by tying a stick to one end of a piece of string, and a magnet to the other. Cut several fish shapes 2" to 3" long. Clip a paper clip on each fish.
With the children: Put fish into the container. Children take turns seeing how many "fish" they can catch with the rod.

Variations:

Fishing for apples. Screw large cup hooks into the apples and tie another hook to the end of a line. Try to hook an apple floating in water.

HUCKLE BUCKLE BEANSTALK   **ages 3 and up**

Method:

Choose a small object to hide. Start the game by having everyone cover their eyes while you put the object in a spot that is visible but not conspicuous. The group searches around the room with their hands behind their backs, looking for a glimpse of the object. The minute they see it they look away and say "Huckle Buckle Beanstalk." The game continues until everyone has seen the object. The first to see the object is "it" next and rehides the object.

Suggestion:

This is a quick game that can be done easily when there is a gap in time. To vary the playing, you can change the object or room where you're playing.

Music

HIGH AND LOW SOUNDS—NO. 2   ages 4 and up

Materials:

record player

records—"Do-Re-Mi" from *Sound of Music* or others you may choose to fit the activity.

Method:

Sing or play the song "Do-Re-Mi" and show the children that your voice goes from low to high. Use your hand to show high and low sounds as you sing. Let the children imitate you with their hands.

TART TIN SHAKERS   ages 4 and up

These make great maracas for rhythm band!

Materials:

matching tart tins—2 per child

wooden picnic spoons—2 per child

small supply of shaking material such as dry beans, macaroni, rice or dried cereals (the last is best in case an adventurous child tries to sample)

peel-off stickers or gummed paper for decorating the finished shakers

scissors

stapler

Method:

The children place some shaking material in one tin. Help them place the other tin on top and staple closely ¾ of the way around. Insert the two spoons opposite each other bowl side in (tongue depressors slip out too easily) and finish stapling.

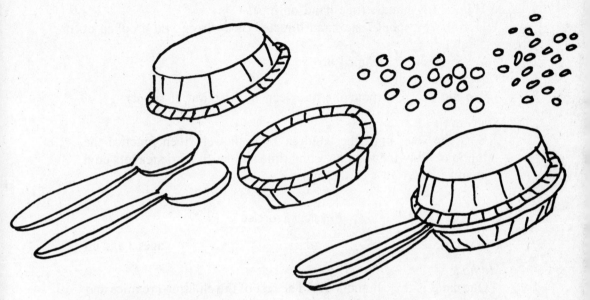

Suggestion:

These do not need to be decorated, but available materials are suggested to keep the children occupied while waiting for their turn with you and the stapler.

Variation:

Paper pie plates also make good shakers and may be made in the same way. Some might prefer to sew the plates together with needle and colorful yarn instead of stapling.

TEAPOT SONG AND DANCE   **ages 3 and up**

Verse:
   I'm a little teapot short and stout (point to self)
   Here is my handle (one hand on hip)
   Here is my spout (one hand directed away from you crooked at
   elbow)
   When I get all steamed up
   Hear me shout
   Tip me over and pour me out (lean in direction of spout)

Suggestion:
   Sing the song until the children know it well, then practice the
   motions. Play the song a second time and let the little teapots do a
   creative dance just to the music.

Physical Exercise

CAT AND MICE   **ages 3 and up**

Method:
   One child is the cat and hides. The rest of the children are mice and
   sneak up to the cat's hiding place and scratch. This is the signal for
   the cat to chase the mice and try to catch one. Then choose another
   child to be the cat. The game continues until everyone has had a
   turn to be cat. Background music adds to the fun of this game.

PAPER PUNCHING BAG   **ages 4 and up**

Materials:
   medium-sized bags (paper or plastic)
   old newspapers
   string
   scissors

Method:
   Children "scrunch up" pieces of newspaper and stuff the paper
   bags. Tie each securely shut with a piece of string long enough so
   that the bag may be hung. One or more bags are hung and the
   children punch until the bags break apart or until the children tire
   of the activity. Bags can be hung from a clothesline, basement pipe,

screw eye or cup hook, or they can be secured on a smooth ceiling with heavy tape.

Comment:

This idea came from four-year-old Craig, who has done it several times with friends. It has a surprising fascination and works off a lot of energy.

Science

MAGNIFYING MAGIC   ages 3 and up

Materials:

large variety of living and nonliving things
    examples: ant, worm, wool material, sandpaper, sugar
good magnifying glass for each child.

Method:

Give the children plenty of time to look at as many as they wish. Talk about the difference the glass makes and which object they each felt changed the most when it was magnified.

Suggestions:

Let them explore other objects around the room. Go outside and investigate objects—insect life, bark, bricks, etc.

BIRDSEED PICTURES IN THE SNOW   ages 3 and up

Materials:

bag of birdseed for each child

Method:

Encourage the children to make designs in the snow by sprinkling birdseed—circles, letters, numbers, abstractions, a face, etc. Now the birds can dine on them!

Storytelling

ONE STORY THREE WAYS   ages 4 and up

Materials:

appropriate stories: *Jack and the Beanstalk; Katy and the Big Snow,* V. Burton; *The Little House,* V. Burton

record player

record of same story

Method:

The idea is that the children become more aware of how the same story can be told differently and still mean the same. The first time you do this you might start with a short story they already know and love. Let them look the book over by themselves before you play the record, then ask a child to tell his interpretation of the same story.

Suggestion:

After you have done this with several stories, discuss which they enjoy best—the reading, listening or telling.

Trips

GOING TO SEE A FLORIST   **ages 3 and up**

A nearby florist will welcome little visitors during the quiet season between Christmas and Easter. A midwinter breath of spring!

Method:

Call ahead and plan with the florist for a visiting day. The children will first of all love seeing and smelling flowers when it's still very much winter outside. They will also want to watch the florist make an arrangement and hear how the flowers travel to his shop and what kind of refrigerators he has for keeping them fresh.

Suggestions:

If it is the right time, perhaps you could buy some white stones and narcissus bulbs to plant in paper cups when you get home.

Woodworking

SAWING CARDBOARD   **ages 3 and up**

A very good early sawing experience!

Materials:

cardboard pieces from corrugated cardboard boxes
hacksaw or coping saw
vise
masking or Scotch tape

Method:

Let the children saw the cardboard into pieces. They may then enjoy taping the pieces together to make abstract shapes.

Suggestions:

1. More sophisticated four-year-olds may enjoy sawing "windows" and "doors" from a cardboard box "house," using tape for hinges. (Boxes that major appliances come in are good for this.)
2. An exceptionally well-coordinated child may hold a cardboard piece on a low table with a hand and knee, sawing with the other hand and forgetting the vise altogether.

MARCH

March Contents

March Guideposts

Things You Can Collect

It is March! You and the children experience a growing sense of excitement. The sun is warmer, melting the snow more quickly after each new storm. Nature gives dozens of other reminders that there are warmer days to come. This month offers its own special set of collectibles.

TREASURES UNDER THE SNOW

For the sake of sheer whimsy, plan a trek with the children to find "treasures" under the melting snow. You will see fresh green things beginning to peep up. Unforeseen surprises will add spice to the hunt. Sharon may find an old mitten. Eric may emerge from behind a bush with a long lost frisbee. A penny may appear in the gutter. What an exciting game for a playgroup collecting session!

PUSSY WILLOW

Now is the time for you to cut a few pussy willow branches. Perhaps the "pussies" are already visible on the stalks. Have them ready so each child can take at least one sprig home to put in water and enjoy indoors.

BUDS TO FORCE

This is the month, too, for forcing some early blooms or greenery. A favorite, of course, is forsythia, because of its brilliant yellow blossoms. Quince works well also. For that matter, almost any branch you see that has leaf buds can be snipped and encouraged to produce foliage in a glass of water. Explicit directions are in the March science section.

BUGS

Are you a biologist deep down? Pop a few early insects into a jar for later examination indoors. Maybe you are equipped with an identification book. Children love to see the real thing and compare it with a picture. A variety of bugs can often be found in swarms jumping about on the snow in woodland areas as spring nears.

EGGSHELLS

Indoors, you can begin setting aside eggshells. Save whole ones, painstakingly blown out, which can be used for egg painting and other decoration. (Prick a hole in each end. Blow through one end while the egg emerges from the other into a waiting dish for later scrambling.) Half shells will be perfect "plant pots" for seed germination. See the EGGSHELL FACES project in the March science section. Crushed shells can be painted or dyed and used alone or with other bits (paper, fabric, etc.) for designs. Glue on almost any kind of surface—stones, boxes, sheets of paper.

EASTER OR ST. PATRICK'S COOKIE CUTTERS

If the kitchen remains your favorite workshop for family and playgroup projects, it can be cookie time again. Find cutters in bunny and other Easter shapes, shamrocks for St. Patrick's day, too. Keep in mind that the cutters remain excellent for play dough projects. What about dough tinted green for cutting out and drying a shamrock to take home to Dad?

Remember the Familiar

SIGNS OF SPRING

The neighbor couple on their daily stroll, members of many classrooms, the reporter for the local paper—everyone is looking for signs of spring! See what your preschoolers can notice—crocus blooms, a robin, leaf buds, a great big worm. On your return from a walk you could let the children review their findings as you print their words on a piece of paper. Read their "story" out loud to them. Print small copies so each one has one to take home.

OUTSIDE PLAY EQUIPMENT

It is not too soon to put up the outside play equipment. The first days of climbing and swinging after the long winter are especially exciting.

MARCH WINDS

After an invigorating outdoor playtime you might read a poem or two about windy March days. Talk about what the wind is like. It is . . . "cold," "loud," "strong," "fast." It makes . . . "the trees bend," "dry leaves rustle," "cheeks pink."

ST. PATRICK'S DAY

Mid-March brings St. Patrick's Day when everyone is Irish! Remind the mothers to let the children wear something green. *You* wear something green. Have green snacks—limeade, green cookies. Do projects in green. Make green hats. Frost crackers or cookies green. Decorate green placemats. Leaf through the months for other activities that can be "turned green."

SEASONAL MUSIC AND OTHER SONGS

Put on a few records of sprightly Irish music to dance to or as background music for snacks and projects. Then wind up singing a nursery rhyme just for fun.

EARLY EASTER

If this is the year when Easter and Passover are celebrated early, turn to April's activities for special ideas.

March *does* have a great deal to offer. Pick your favorites and enjoy them with your family or preschoolers.

March Activities

Arts and Crafts

FUZZY ANIMALS   ages 3 and up

Materials:
scissors
precut animal shape (large—from 9"x12" or larger paper)
variety of soft and fuzzy materials such as:
yarn
felt
cotton
pieces of carpet sample
discarded fur
pieces of fake fur, etc.
glue and brushes

Method:
Children cut and glue the "fuzzies" to the animal shapes. For example: cotton body, yarn hair or tail, felt eyes. Let the children pick their own combinations.

Variations:
Make "feelies" using a variety of textures such as sandpaper, wet-look wallpaper, styrofoam plates, etc. These can be in a special shape or a collage.

BURLAP GIFTS PAINTED WITH LOVE   ages 4 and up

Burlap-covered wastebaskets, pencil holders and mail-holders make useful gifts and make the child's art important to him

Materials:
orange juice cans for pencil holders
inexpensive dime-store mail-holders
or
inexpensive wastepaper baskets

enough burlap to cover the number of items needed
glue applied with appropriate-size brush
scissors
brightly colored braid to finish around the top and bottom of the item
poster paints (thick cream consistency)
paintbrushes

Method:

Before children come: Cover the outer surface of each item with glue and then press the burlap to fit. It is difficult to cut the burlap to exact size, but once glued to the object it can easily be trimmed with a single-edged razor. A damp cloth will be helpful for wiping away excess glue.

After the children come: Let them paint free designs on the covered containers with several bright colors. When this dries, you will help them measure and glue the braid trim around the top and bottom.

Suggestions:

1. Burlap contact paper is more expensive, but can be used in place of glue and burlap yard goods.

2. Encourage the children to keep their paint colors separate to avoid a muddy effect.

Variation:

Burlap Wall Hanging—The children are given a precut piece of burlap with a coat hanger or dowel inserted and stitched secure in the top hem for hanging. The children can fringe the sides and bottom then paint on a design. Abstracts are most effective as the roughness of burlap makes details difficult.

Too dry a paintbrush will make it difficult to design your wall hanging, and yet too much paint will curl the burlap. Give the children an extra brush for each color to avoid rinsing one in water between colors. Stapling the burlap onto cardboard before painting helps prevent curling.

HINGED ABSTRACTIONS   ages 3 and up

Materials:

brass paper fasteners
cardboard, construction paper, oaktag, posterboard (any or all)
scissors
one-hole punch (optional)

Method:

Children cut pieces of paper, oaktag etc., and push fasteners through to hook one piece to another. You help make holes for fasteners with scissors or punch.

The result will be an abstract object with a number of moving parts.

Variation:
Predraw and cut arms, legs, body and head of person, animal or Halloween skeleton, etc. Punch holes for fasteners to go through. Children put parts together with fasteners. You might also provide crayons for adding features.

RESIST PAINTING   **ages 4 and up**

Materials:
white paper 9"x12"—1 per child
crayons
poster paint (black or other dark color very effective)
brushes

Method:
Children draw with crayons, making marks by pressing very hard; then paint over all marks and bare area. The crayon will resist the paint, giving an interesting effect.

Suggestions:
1. Use bright-colored crayons to make autumn leaves. Then paint with blue or black to get effect of cold autumn day. (A series of colored spots make great "leaves.")
2. Use white crayons to make snowflakes (spots again!), snowmen etc. Paint black for a wintry night effect.
3. Underwater scenes: bright colored fish and plants, blue or green paint.

SHAVING-CREAM PAINTING   **ages 3 and up**

Materials:
aerosol spray can of shaving cream
cleared-off table top (covered with plastic or oil cloth to protect)

Method:
Help children spray cream on the table.
Children draw pictures in the cream with their fingers and hands.

Variation:
   Hungry children would enjoy this idea using cooled chocolate or butterscotch pudding instead of shaving cream.

Cooking

SHAKING AND BAKING CHICKEN   ages 3 and up

Materials:
   1 package of coating for baking chicken by the shaker-bag method
   drumsticks—enough for the group

Method:
   Allow each child to shake one or two drumsticks of his own and to place them on the baking pan. Bake at 400° for 40-50 minutes and serve as part of the children's lunch.

SUGAR ON SNOW   ages 3 and up

Materials:
   individual small pie plates or tart tins—1 per child
   fresh clean snow or shaved ice
   butter
   maple syrup
   candy thermometer
   forks
   optional: hot biscuits or sour pickles

Method:
   Fill up the individual pie plates or tart tins with packed new snow or shaved ice. Butter the rim of a large cooking pot and boil syrup to 232°F on candy thermometer (without thermometer just let it get to a good rolling boil). Pour syrup over each child's snow or ice. With forks the children twirl taffy like strips. Eat it plain or with hot biscuits and/or sour pickles—believe it or not!

Dramatic Play

MIDWINTER DAY AT THE BEACH   ages 3 and up

An indoor, down-in-the-basement pursuit!

Materials:
  any or all of these:
    beach bags
    towels   You can ask the children to bring these.
    bag lunches
    pans of water with shells and stones
    tub of sand with containers and digging equipment (shovels, scoops, spoons)
    a play boat (real inflatable one, cardboard or packing box one with stick mast and pillowcase or posterboard sail)

Method:
  Ahead of time: Prepare the above and anything else you can think of to add to the atmosphere (tape a big cheery cutout of the sun to your front door).
  With the children: Let them play-act "A Summer Day at the Beach." Include a picnic in the boat or on beach towels.

SITUATION GAME   ages 3 and up

Method:
  Sit in a circle together and talk about one or more of these emergency situations. Ask what the children would do if . . .
    a strange man offered you chewing gum and a ride home
    baby brother ate some cleaner, a bottle of pills, or a toadstool
    your friend fell off his bike and couldn't move
    you were eating a picnic and saw a hungry child
    found an injured bird
    found an injured squirrel (danger of rabies)
    found fire in your house
    (You may think of others)

As the children express their ideas, you can add practical suggestions on how to cope with the problem.

TAPE RECORDER SHOW AND TELL   ages 3 and up

Materials:
  tape recorder

Method:

Optional: Ahead of time tell parents to have their children choose
something special to bring and tell about.

With the children: Record the voices on tape as they tell about the
object they have brought to show or about the exciting thing that
happened recently. Replay.

The children will be hesitant at first but warm up to it as they
hear their own voices.

Suggestions:

1. Ideas for things to bring:
   treasure from summer vacation
   favorite toy from birthday, Chanukah or Christmas
   item from recent trip or outing
2. Help them by asking questions about their experience.
3. Record other things of interest:
   songs you sing and other music activities
   stories you make up together
   puppet conversations
   children's comments about what they liked best after a play
      group trip
   the group doing a finger game together, etc.
   all kinds of "tell us about" activities

Games

BEACH STONE GAMES   ages 3 and up

Method:

Beach stones are fun to play with, touch and sort. In water their
colors become more brilliant. They are a pleasant reminder of
summer and can be the start of many simple and effective games.
Be sure you have an ample and varied supply for each child.

Suggest—

  counting games
  sorting by colors
  big—bigger—biggest
  hiding games
  guessing games (which one is missing?)
  designs with stones

Let them see if they can work out a simple game pattern from any one of these ideas. They may want to include others or play by themselves. Have a pan of water available. They will have a good time just putting the stones in and playing.

Suggestion:
Sometime when the children have been for a walk and picked field flowers show them how you can put beach stones in the bottom of a jar of water to help hold the flower arrangement in place.

NAME GAME   ages 4 and up

Children just love this. It is well worth your effort

Materials:
enough multicolored poster board to cut out each child's name in *very* large individual letters—12"-18" high—for economy, use heavy brown wrapping paper or cut-up shopping bags
pencil
ruler
scissors
magic markers or crayons

Method:
Ahead of time: Draw letters block style. Cut out. Hide each child's name in a different room, each letter tucked in a special hiding place.
With the children: Have children help each other find their letters—one room, one child's name at a time. Help children spread out their letters in proper order on the floor. Some will know how; others may recognize their letters but not know the proper order. You may give each child a piece of paper with his name printed on it as a guide to this letter arranging.
   Children may decorate their letters with magic marker or crayon.
   They may practice mixing up the letters and laying them out again.

Variation:
When all the children know the letters (not necessarily in order) to their own names, put all the letters in a pile and mix them up.

Everyone sits in a circle around them. Each child takes a turn finding one letter from his name. When everyone has all his letters, the children assemble them in proper order on the floor.

Suggestion:
You may save the letters at your house to be used similarly on other occasions—or send them home with the children.

TABLE HOCKEY   ages 4 and up

A rainy-day invention of two 7-year-old boys

Materials:
2 cardboard tubes from paper toweling (or 1 for each child playing)
1 plastic lid
a large table

Method:
The boys had fun decorating and personalizing their own paper toweling tubes. Then they positioned themselves at opposite ends of the table and began shooting the plastic lid back and forth. If it went off a side of the table no points were scored, but a shot off the table end where your partner is standing made a goal and scored a point for you.

Suggestion:
This game could be played without points and with 4 children or more. The object of the game then would be to see how long the children could keep the lid from going off the table.

Comment:
When the boys finished the game, they used their tubing sticks to dip in soap suds for blowing extra-large bubbles.

Music

MUSIC BOXES—PLAY AND LISTEN   ages 3 and up

Materials:
 any variety of music boxes or musical gadgets
 examples:
   musical stuffed toy

> musical teapot
> baby's pull-cord music box
> musical Christmas tree
> small boxes with revolving figures on top
> jewel box
> old-fashioned, crank type music box

Method:

Let the children wind, turn, pull, etc. to make the music boxes play ... one box and one child at a time.

Suggestions:

1. This is special fun if you do it while having cocoa together out of a musical tea- or coffee-pot.
2. You may request ahead of time that each child bring a musical object or toy if he has one.

MUSICAL HANDS AND FEET   ages 3 and up

Rhythm—Long and short values

Materials:

2 pieces of paper per child, about 8"x11"
black crayon or pencil
scissors
masking tape

Method:

Have the children rhythmically chant the poem *Hot Cross Buns*. It should have the following long and short values.

Hot cross buns	= short, short, long	= ♩♩ 𝅗𝅥
Hot cross buns	= short, short, long	= ♩♩ 𝅗𝅥
One-a-penny, two-a-penny	= very quickly	= ♫♫ ♫♫
Hot cross buns.	= short, short, long	= ♩♩ 𝅗𝅥

Trace each child's foot (left and right) on separate pieces of paper. Cut out the paper feet. (Your expert 4-year-old cutters may help with this.) Tape them to the floor. Have the children stand on their "paper feet" and chant and clap the rhythm. Then let them try just stamping the rhythm.

Variation:
Let two stamp and two clap, alternating each verse.

WATER GLASS MUSICAL—NO. 2   ages 3 and up

Materials:
3 identical glasses or bottles
a spoon
1 small pitcher of water

Method:
Ahead of time: Experiment with the water and glasses to be sure you can get the three glasses to sound the first three tones of the song *Three Blind Mice* (mi-re-do).
With the children: Leave the glasses empty. Let the children watch and listen as you experiment, testing different amounts of water in the glasses to get the *Three Blind Mice* tones again. Sing the words "three blind mice" with the children as you tap the three glasses.
  Using the glasses, ask questions about how the sound is changing—going up, going down.
  Is this sound (strike a glass) higher than this sound (strike another)?
  Does the sound go up or down? (Strike two notes)
  etc.
  Let each child strike two or three notes and talk about whether the sound went up or down. The listeners may use their hands to move up or down with the sound of the note.

Physical Exercise

CIRCLE GAME   ages 3 and up

Materials:
string or masking tape

Method:

Make a circle on the floor with string or tape. Tape works well even on carpeting. Everyone gathers around the circle. Children take turns saying what to do—"Run around the circle" . . . "hop," "jump," "crawl around," etc. Everyone follows the directions till you call on another child for a new idea for what to do.

Variations:

The circle game lends itself to music activities. For example: marching music, hopping music, music that makes you think of something special, may be used as children move around the circle.

CLOTHESPIN AND BOTTLE GAME   ages 4 and up

Eye-hand coordination

Materials:

clothespins, handful of pencils, crayons, or other substitute
large wide-mouthed jar, empty oatmeal container or any similar
    container

Method:

Children take turns standing over the container and trying to drop the clothespins in.

Comment:

A milk bottle, while fine for older children, may have too narrow an opening for the skill of a 3- or 4-year-old.

Science

FORCING BUDS   ages 3 and up

Materials:

any plant, bush or tree that has buds on its branches (pussy willow,
    forsythia, rhododendron, etc.)
scissors
container

Method:

Take a walk with the children to look for buds. Clip enough for each child to have a sprig or two to take home. Place in water till children are ready to leave, then send home with instructions for care—"sunny spot, put in container of water, can transplant in soil when roots form."

Suggestion:

Talk with the children about how plants need food and water like we do. Talk about how they take nourishment through roots. They will "send out" longer and longer roots to "look" for food.

EGGSHELL FACES WITH GRASS HAIR   ages 4 and up

Materials:

eggshells with top part off—1 per child
soil (better when mixed with a little vermiculite, available at dime
    stores and nurseries)

grass seed
magic marker
egg cups or sections cut from egg cartons
spoons

Method:

Children spoon soil into eggshell which is sitting in an egg cup or carton section. They draw a face on the shell with the markers. They sprinkle in the seeds. You water the soil lightly and send the project home with the children with instructions for keeping the seeds and soil constantly damp, not flooded, by watering.

Suggestion:

A collar to hold the eggshell head may be made by trimming the top and bottom of an egg carton section, or by taping together a circlet of construction paper.

Variation:

Using undecorated egg shells, make an eggshell garden, planting any type of seeds desired. Growing roots may break the shell eventually. On another playgroup day it may be pointed out that roots are strong. They push down and out in the soil as they grow. Big tree roots can break a sidewalk.

TASTING TELLS   ages 3 and up

Materials:

small dish of salt
small dish of sugar
2 identical glass pitchers
water
paper cups or spoons for tasting

Method:

Ahead of time: Set out the dishes of salt and sugar. Fill one pitcher with some water and add salt. Fill the second pitcher with the same amount of water and add sugar.

With the children: Show the children salt in one dish and sugar in another. Ask what it is. How can you find out? Since you don't see a difference taste it. Do the pitchers look the same? How can we make sure? Have some taste one and the rest the other. Exchange.

What was the difference in the water? Be sure to stress that we do not taste things without knowing it's safe to do so.

Variation:
Try comparing two different flavors of Jell-o dissolved in water but not yet jelled. Blindfold the children and let them sample. Taste tells the difference. Give them each the flavored water to drink then repeat the experience with their noses blocked. What happens when you have a cold?

SIGNS OF SPRING WALK   ages 3 and up

Materials:
bags for everyone—for "treasure" collecting

Method:
Tell children they are going on a walk—a special treasure hunt—to see if little plants are beginning to grow now that winter is over.
You might ask, "What happens outside when winter is over?" Responses might be, "Snow melts." "Leaves come on the trees." "Flowers grow."
You help by telling them things to look for:
    bugs and small creatures appearing
    buds on bushes and trees
    green coming through the ground
    birds
"Let's see how many things we can find."
Examine: the garden, nearby woods, edge of a pond or stream

Remember:
Be good ecologists. Leave things as you find them. Confine your collecting largely to stones, twigs, fallen items.

Storytelling

MY BOOK OF COLORS   ages 3 and up

Materials:
plain paper (approximately 9"x12")—four or more pages per child
    depending on how many colors will be represented in the book
    (halve sheets if you wish)
hole punch
brass fasteners or string

colored paper, crayons, magic marker, and/or cut-outs of objects in
colors that will be shown in the book
scissors
glue and brushes

Method:

Ahead of time: Punch holes in the "pages." Cut out a number of
colored pictures—green dress, yellow umbrella, red house, etc.
Make a "title" page for each child with "My Book of Colors" and
the child's name printed on it.

With the children: Explain that each child is going to make his
very own book about colors. Give everyone a sheet of paper. You
choose a color, or let each person decide which one he wishes to do.

Then:

If the color is *red* let everyone
   —snip a piece of *red* paper and glue it on the page
   —make a *red* line or picture with the crayon or marker
   —glue a *red* cut-out to the page

One or all of these may be done. If there is a wide range of ability
in your group some may do one of these; others, all of them.

Proceed to the other colors. Help the children fasten together
completed pages. Write the proper color name on each page—best
printing, please.

Remember:

Some children may do as little as a part of one page. Fasten the
empty pages with the completed ones; put a few materials in a
plastic bag, giving the child a wonderful project kit to take home for
working on his book when Mom or Dad has a minute to help.

Variations:

Do other "My Book of ———" projects.
Examples: shapes, animals, cars, numbers, transportation, letters,
clothes, foods, birds, plants.

Trips

RIDE ON A TRAIN (BUS, SUBWAY, STREETCAR)   ages 3 and up

Method:

Choose a point of departure, destination and point of return that fit
into your time schedule. At the destination, you might stop for an
ice cream treat, but the real point is the ride itself.

Discuss as you go:
   1. Schedules: the idea that the bus or train comes and goes at a special time.
   2. Fare: a ticket must be purchsed or money put in a slot (children may do this).
   3. Conductor (or driver): collects the fare, helps his passengers with any problem that might arise.
   4. Station (or stop): where passengers get on and off; may be marked by a building, a shelter, or simply a sign, as in the case of many bus stops.

Woodworking

HAMMERING YOUR NAME   ages 4 and up

Materials:
   hammer
   very large nail or spike
   sanded piece of soft wood long enough for the child's name
   pencil

Method:
   With the pencil you or the children lightly print their names in large letters. Then with the spike and hammer they pound or, more accurately, tap a series of holes along the letter lines.

Suggestions:
   1. This is a good exercise in hammering coordination, as a spike head is large and it does not take long to make each indentation. The closer together the holes are made, the more clearly the letters will show.
   2. Some children might rather make designs than names.

SAW-IT-YOURSELF PUZZLE   **ages 4 and up**

Materials:
   one piece of balsa wood per child
   approximately 6"x7"x1"
   (Use of corrugated cardboard is also appropriate, especially for 3-
      year-old groups.)
         or

simple shape precut by Mother or Daddy with a coping or electric
    saw (heart, duck, triangle, etc.)
vise or C-clamp
hack saw
optional: magic markers, paint and brushes for coloring the puzzle

Note:
Balsa may be obtained at a hobby shop or lumber store. It often
comes in precut blocks or sheets. Choose something not too thick,
close to the size you want or get a sheet and cut it into pieces of the
correct size when you get home. Buy the cheapest grade.

Method:
Ahead of time: If you are using precut shapes, saw the wood
pieces into the shapes of your choice.
With the children: Let the children take turns at the vise sawing
their wood into just two or three pieces. (simple, fairly straight
lines)
Optional:
The children then color their puzzle pieces. You may prefer to let
some or all of the children color the wood before sawing. One child
might saw while the others color while awaiting their turns.

Suggestions:
1. Allow time for playing with the puzzles. The children might
enjoy trying one another's.
2. Have some plastic sandwich bags handy in which each child may
carry his puzzle.

APRIL

April Contents

April Guideposts

Things You Can Collect

Perhaps this month is bringing more showers than flowers when you had been anticipating that first taste of true spring weather. Springlike activities can be planned for both inside and out. Rain need not dampen anyone's enthusiasm—put on your happy face! Think spring and collect for spring.

WHITE SHELLED EGGS

Maybe March slipped by without your collecting a single egg. Get busy and whip up a few egg dishes for your family and save the blown-out or cracked shells. Hardboil a batch of white eggs in vinegared water and tuck them in the "fridge" for later dyeing projects.

If you are both ambitious and artistic, use your imagination for painting or further embellishing fragile hollow shells to hang on bare branches for an egg tree. Use your handiwork as a centerpiece for a special playgroup Easter party and for your own family's enjoyment.

April offers other opportunities for dipping into undone March egg projects. The EGGSHELL FACES offer a delightful variation of the Easter egg theme. If you prefer, take time this month to let the children crush the broken eggshells and glue to various surfaces for primitive mosaics. Shells can be colored by you or the children either before or after the gluing, for varying effects. Magic marker, water colors and crayon all offer means for ornamentation. Do you envision results to rival intricate Roman design? A few pieces affixed to a surface with a dash of bright color represents work ambitious enough for the preschool set.

Simply dyeing hard-boiled eggs is forever a favorite. Use the kits available at the grocer's or the food coloring already handy in your kitchen cupboard. One trick is to crayon on a name or design before spoon-dipping the egg into food coloring and water. The result is very effective. Maybe one of the small fry would like to see what happens if you mix different dye colors together. What a perfect time to learn about colors with a little controlled experimentation.

STICKERS

If dyeing seems too messy an undertaking, whip out crayons or stickers for a tidier means of achieving colorful results. The stickers will lend a pretty decoupage effect. Some youngsters may enjoy seeing their very own name or initial on an egg. Alphabet stickers or crayons can turn that trick most successfully.

You will want to include the seasonal holiday theme in your sticker supply. Have an assortment of bunnies, chicks and the like for making cards, putting on packages or dressing up plain napkins and paper cups for a special holiday party.

One helpful hint to remember is that preschoolers find the peel-and-stick variety easier to use. Licking a sticker without removing the glue can be tricky business for some children.

COTTON BALLS

Set aside some cotton balls for this season's projects, too. The fuzzy round tufts can make a bunny appear on almost anything! Your preschoolers will take delight in creating a picture of bunnies hiding in the grass—an effect easily achieved on drawing paper with a few quick strokes of green crayon for grass and several dots of glue atop which the youngsters pop their cotton balls. You even have the perfect chance for a little number play. "See, the bunnies couldn't hide their tails, so we can count how many are hiding in each child's picture!"

TUNA CANS

If you save enough tuna cans and cover them with felt, you can help the children make three-dimensional bunnies. The cotton balls come in handy again as bunny tails. Paper, felt, marker—any combination of materials—can be used as the children create the face and whiskers at the opposite end of the can. Put on paper ears and—presto!—there is a bunny which can double as a good jellybean container.

BABY LEAVES

If that spring-fever weather you had hoped for does happen along you can have a breath of fresh air with your group as you go out to inspect the green mist wrapping the trees and discover tiny, fragile leaves which, in their adulthood, will be the sturdy leaves of summer. Talk about how they will grow up. Point out how you all saw leaf buds on these very same trees during your midwinter walks. Let everyone have a sprig to show Mother. Make a collection to press in a heavy book on the return from your walk. Miniature oak, maple and other leaves, a few tiny pressed flowers, can be put under contact paper to make bookmarks, cards, a small hanging, or other projects, now or later.

Remember the Familiar

APRIL SHOWERS

What child doesn't love raindrops and puddles? Bundle up in weather proof clothing, pull out gaily colored umbrellas—Daddy-sized black ones, too—and set out for some puddle-jumping and maybe even a little tricycle-riding in the rain.

As you are enjoying your wet weather spree someone may notice how the once-dead winter ground is now covered with a haze of green. Take a minute to talk about how rain helps things grow, and how warmer weather is continuing to bring more things to life.

Somehow certain children lose all sense of perspective when confronted with a puddle! Your outing could well turn into an impromptu splash party. Be prepared with a few extras in the way of dry clothing. In spite of rain gear someone will have managed to get thoroughly soaked! Be ready, too, with cups of soup or cocoa to warm the memory of good fun.

The rainy day is the perfect one for drawing rain pictures or making "drip" paintings. Some children might have stories they would like to tell about their rain pictures. If someone does several papers staple them together and show the resulting "rain book" to the others. The colorful pictures may even lead to making a poem together about colored rain. You can be the secretary and write it down.

This would be the time to play a little "rain" music as a background while you do your projects. Learn a "rain" song together or read the group a selection of "rain" poetry.

EASTER EGG HUNT

What child does not like an Easter egg hunt? Supply your preschoolers with a bag for collecting, or supply egg cartons cut down with a handle added. Quart vegetable and fruit baskets or even small pails made from liquid bleach bottles (see May collecting ideas) are equally useful. Fill each with paper "grass." The same containers will double for carrying the results of the egg dyeing or cooking projects.

Have your little ones seek colored hard-boiled eggs that you have concealed. For extra appeal, send them on a quest for jellybeans tucked in the grass or treat-filled plastic eggs that you have buried in the sandbox. Remember to hide the eggs in a partially visible fashion if they are spread about over a wide area.

Before the hunt begins state a few simple rules. Set limits so all the children will end up with an equal quantity of booty. You do not want to be confronted by one triumphant preschooler determinedly guarding his own vast hoard while the others wail that they did not get their share. One solution is to tell them what their quota will be. When a child finds his allotment, he proceeds to help someone else who is having difficulty.

If the weather is not balmy or dry enough for an outdoor hunt simply switch operations to the confines of the house.

PLAY DOUGH AND CLAY AT PASSOVER AND EASTER

If you lacked time to prepare for something elaborate as an egg hunt, the old standbys, play dough or clay, can lend themselves to seasonal activities. What about making "eggs" from the colored materials to put in Easter baskets, or readying for a pretend Passover feast by shaping matzos?

Enjoy those first warm sunny days. April suggests a myriad of exciting possibilities for fun with your preschoolers. Turn rainy days into indoor and outdoor adventures as you bid goodbye to winter's final remnants and welcome spring's first signs.

April Activities

Arts and Crafts

DRAWING FROM LIFE   ages 4 and up

This increases powers of observation.

Materials:
  crayons
  paper (9"x12")
  a familiar object with basic shape and color
  For a first experience choose something round such as:
    apple
    orange
    ball
    balloon
  If everyone has one object of his own to keep touching, the activity
is even more successful.

Method:
  Let everyone hold the object. Talk together about its roundness or
straightness. Talk about its color. Put the object in the center of the
table. Give out art materials and let the children draw it. Let them
make more than one drawing on the paper. Encourage their making
the object big.

Suggestions:
  1. A child may well simply have an orange-colored scribble for his
orange, but at least he understands the "orangeness" of the fruit, if
not its shape. After the discussion let your artists "do their own
thing".
  2. Lend importance to the finished product by printing a title
("Oranges") and artist's name on it. Mount on a larger colored
sheet.

Variations:
1. Use the activity on other occasions. Progress to rectangular or triangular shapes, perhaps colored blocks. Later use two simple objects at a time or an object made up of two shapes, as in a lollipop.
2. Try round objects again, but use clay or play dough.

FISHBOWL WITHOUT WATER   ages 3 and up

Materials:
glass jars (honey jars and other jars with rounded sides are great)
fish—pictures cut from magazines or from colored paper
glue and brushes
choice of:

moss	shells	plastic greenery
pebbles	fake pearls	air-growing greenery
sand		from the florist

Method:
Children glue fish onto outside of glass; then put in shells, pebbles, greenery, etc.
  Fish stickers would make it easier for the 3-year-olds to do this independently.

MAY DAY BASKETS   ages 3 and up

Materials:
paper plates—1 per child
ribbon—about 9 in. per child
scissors
real, artificial or paper flowers and/or:
(see "Paper Flower Bouquet," May activity)
paper butterfly
paper leaves
lollipops
individual sticks of gum
little messages
stapler or tape
pipe cleaner, straws or popsicle stick stems to attach to flowers,
    butterflies, leaves, messages

Method:

Children fold plate in half. You put slit in plate and tape or staple basket shut above slit. Children put ribbon through slit to make handle. You tie bows for children while they insert flowers into the edges of the basket. You may use stapler to make flowers more secure.

MONOPRINT WITH FINGERPAINT   **ages 3 and up**

Materials:

liquid starch (in discarded dish-detergent container for ease in pouring)

poster paint in powdered form (in flour shakers for best control)

white shelf paper—cut in pieces 9"x12" or larger

formica table top or other well-protected surface (use paper if you wish)

Method:

Either you or the children pour a small amount of starch on the work surface; shake on color and mix with hands. Children make designs with fingers.

Help each press paper onto a design to make an imprint on the paper. You may do this two or three times with the same piece of paper using a different color for each addition.

The result is a superimposed picture with a silk-screen appearance.

Cooking

COCONUT PASTEL BONBONS   ages 3 and up

No cooking!

Materials:
cookie sheet
waxed paper
mixing bowl
beaters
Recipe ingredients:
1 3 oz. pkg. cream cheese, *softened*
2 ¹/₂ c. confectionery sugar
¹/₄ t. vanilla
dash salt
food coloring
1 cup grated coconut

Method:
As soon as children come:
Beat cream cheese until soft and smooth. Beat in confectionery sugar gradually until thoroughly blended. Beat in vanilla, salt and food coloring. Let the children take turns adding ingredients and beating. Cover and refrigerate.
One hour later:
Have the children shape the dough into small balls and roll in a plate full of the grated coconut. Line the cookie sheet with waxed paper and put the finished bonbon balls on that. Refrigerate for several hours.

Variation:
Omit food coloring, and instead of coconut, roll in 1 cup chopped nuts.

CINNAMON TOAST DONE WITH COOKIE CUTTERS   ages 3 and up

Materials:
day-old bread
cookie cutters
mixture of cinnamon and sugar (white or brown)—1 ½ tsp. cinnamon to ½ c. sugar or to taste
softened butter
blunt knives or butter spreaders

Method:
Toast bread on one side under the broiler before children cut it with cookie cutters. Let them butter their shapes and sprinkle with cinnamon mixture. Toast under the broiler.

ICE CREAM CONE CUPCAKES   ages 3 and up

Materials:
flat-bottomed waffle ice cream cones
cupcake mix
mixing bowl
beaters
spatula and spoon
frosting
colored sprinkles
bread and butter knives

Method:
Ahead of time (best to do a day ahead): Heat oven to 400°. Make batter for cupcakes as directed on cake mix package. Place the waffle cones on a cookie sheet and fill a scant ½ full (about ¼ cup batter). If you put in too much or too little batter, the cones will not have a nice rounded top. Bake 15-18 min. at 400°. Cool.
With the children: Give the children their own spreading knives and containers of frosting and sprinkles. Let them frost and decorate their cones. For some it may even be more fun than the eating.

Dramatic Play

CHOO-CHOO TRAIN   ages 3 and up

Materials:
  Supply props such as:
    scissors and paper for cutting out "tickets"
    chairs in a line
    a small suitcase or two
    hats, etc.

Method:
  Ask questions such as, "What kinds of people do you see on a
  train?" Let the children choose parts and play "train."
  engineer (can make train sound effects)
  conductor (take tickets, call stations)
  passengers (give tickets, carry luggage)
  redcaps (carry suitcases for passengers)

Suggestions:
  1. This activity can follow a recent train excursion.
  2. If the children are more familiar with bus, airplane, boat or
  other means of transportation, set the scene for playing the familiar
  one.

  Example: Plane Ride—flight attendants pass out lunch, offer
  magazines or blankets and pillows.

CROSSING THE BROOK (OR PUDDLE)   ages 3 and up

An indoor or outdoor game

Materials:
  tape or chalk
  phonograph and records (or use hand clapping)

Method:
  Make lines with tape or chalk to show sides of a "brook". Have the
  children line up behind the leader and cross back and forth over the
  brook, running and jumping to the rhythm of your clapping or the
  recorded music. When the music stops (you control this), whoever
  is caught in the brook must drop out of line and pretend to go home
  to put on dry clothes. Then the child may reenter the game.

GUESS HOW WE FEEL   ages 3 and up

Method:
One child is chosen to go into another room where he cannot hear
the others. The group decides on a mood or feeling—angry, sad, excited, afraid, shy, hurt. Each child has a turn to interpret this in
pantomime—a broken toy, flashlight, unopened box or expressive
picture are unplanned-for items that might help them convey the
feeling to the guesser. More than one answer should be acceptable
—afraid, shy, lonely, or happy, excited, pleased. Give each child a
chance to guess. If someone is timid about doing the pantomime let
him help you think of something in the room for a helpful prop.

Variation:
For older children, the fun of this game might be acting out the feeling as a group.

Games

WATER PLAY   ages 3 and up

Materials:
large container (plastic dishpan, large cooking pot, baby's bathtub,
old tire cut in half horizontally)
water
water toys such as:
  toy boats
  paper cups
  roast baster
  funnel
  plastic containers
  etc.
optional: plastic aprons (also excellent for painting activities)

Method:
You fill the container with water. Place it where spills won't
matter— for example near a drain hole in the cellar floor or even
the bathtub (children can take turns—play two at a time).
  Let children play!

Suggestion:
Great after a messy art project! Put a little soap in the water and
children get clean while playing!

WHAT IS GONE FROM THE TRAY?   ages 3 and up

Materials:
  tray
  5-6 familiar items

Method:
  Children sit in a circle and view the items on the tray. Then they
  hide their eyes. Ask one child to remove one thing from the tray.
  The others open their eyes and try to guess what is missing. The
  game continues until each child has had a chance to remove an
  item.

Suggestions:
  1. Increase the number of items as the game continues.
  2. Vary the items from turn to turn.

Music

MAKING TAMBOURINES   ages 4 and up

Materials:
  paper, styrofoam or disposable plastic plates—2 per child
  beans or macaroni
  stapler or tape
  music (record or singing)

Method:
  Children place a few beans inside one plate and cover it with the
  other plate turned upside-down. Help them staple or tape plates
  securely together.
  Children "play" their instruments tambourine-fashion to the
  music.

Suggestion:
  Easy familiar songs to teach and use for tambourine accompaniment:
    Twinkle Twinkle Little Star
    Do You Know The Muffin Man
    Baa Baa Black Sheep

WATERGLASS MUSICAL NO. 3 **ages 3 and up**

Music Pitch

Materials:
3 glasses or bottles which are the same
3 spoons
1 small pitcher of water

Method:
Ahead of time: Place the three glasses in a row and pour water in each until you have the first three notes of *Three Blind Mice* (mi-re-do).
With the children: Sing *Three Blind Mice* with the children. Show how striking the three glasses in order with the spoon makes the "three blind mice" sound. Let each child try it while you all sing those three words. Let each child try playing as you sing the whole song. The idea is to sound the glasses only when the words "three blind mice" are being sung.

Suggestions:
1. Use the song *Are You Sleeping?* (*Frère Jacques*). This song starts on the lowest tone and goes up (do-re-mi). The child will play only on the words "are you sleep-ing." This will be the low, middle, high and low tones (do-re-mi-do).
2. Use *Old MacDonald Had A Farm.* The words "ee-yi, ee-yi, oh" use the same sounds as *Three Blind Mice*— mi-mi, re-re, do. Play the glasses on "ee-yi, ee-yi, oh."

Helpful hint:
Put hands (and spoon) *all the way behind backs* during parts where you are not supposed to ring the glasses.

Physical Exercise

BALL TOSS GAME **ages 4 and up**

Large-muscle coordination

Materials:
ball, preferably large
1 or more cartons, laundry baskets or other containers

Method:

Line boxes in varying distances from a point where the children have been told to stand. Children take turns throwing the ball, trying to get it into a container. It is "extra special" to get the ball into the box which is farthest away. You may move the point where the children stand farther and farther back to test and increase their skill.

Variation:

Use balloons instead of balls.

PUSSY IN THE CORNER   ages 3 and up

Running game

Method:

Choose one child to stand in the middle of the room while the others select a corner. When you say "Pussy wants a corner," all the children run to different corners and the one in the middle tries to get to a corner. The child left without a corner becomes the one in the middle.

Suggestion:

Make sure no child is "pussy" more than 3 or 4 consecutive turns.

Science

WHAT MAKES THIS SOUND?   ages 3 and up

The senses: Listening—hearing differences in sounds

Materials:
Assemble various objects which will make different kinds of sounds:
  two pieces of wood to strike together
  a metal belt that jangles
  cutlery to strike together
  toss pillows to thump
  cup and saucer
  spoon and glass

Method:
Let children take turns making sounds with the objects as everyone watches and listens. Then, have them cover their eyes as Mother makes a sound and they guess which objects they are hearing. Children take turns making sounds while the others, who have their backs turned or eyes covered, guess.

WHERE DOES FOOD COME FROM?   ages 3 and up

Materials:
  food samples set out on table
    or
  pictures of foods and separate pictures of the foods' sources
  Examples:
    milk—cow—(goat)
    egg—hen
    apple—tree
    hamburger—cattle
    lemon—tree
    pack of frozen peas—plant

Method:
Children tell you where the foods on the table came from or play a game matching pictures of a food and its source.

Suggestion:
1. Precede this activity with a visit to the grocery store. Talk about foods and where they come from as you walk through the store.
2. Take a trip to a poultry or dairy farm

YES OR NO ANIMAL GAME   **ages 3 and up**

Materials:
   glue and brushes
   paper
   pictures of animals (cut out a collection ahead of time)
      and/or
   animal stickers

Method:
   Children stick and paste pictures of animals onto paper. Talk about
   the animals with them as they work (names, how they look).
      Play Yes or No game. You make up statements about the ani-
   mals to which the children say "yes" or "no."
      Examples: Squirrels have bushy tails. "Yes."
                   Elephants have short trunks. "No."
      Some children may be able to make up some statements of their
   own.

Storytelling

STORY OF "ME"   **ages 3 and up**

Materials:
   crayons
   stapler or punch and paper fasteners
   paper—manila sheets about 9"x12"
   pen or magic marker

Method:

Ask children to draw, one at a time:

1. a picture of the family home
2. a picture of brother or sister
3. a picture of a favorite toy or pet

It is important that you pass paper and give directions for each picture singly, allowing the children to complete number 1 before receiving directions and materials for number 2.

As each child finishes a picture, ask him to tell you about it. At the bottom of the picture, write down exactly what he has said about his picture.

Staple the pages together for each child, including a blank front page on which you write the title, "Story of Me," and which the faster children can decorate while the others are finishing up.

Suggestion:

Everyone sits in a circle on the floor while you read each person's book aloud and show the pictures.

EXPERIENCE STORIES   **ages 3 and up**

Materials:

magic marker
large piece of paper
optional: smaller pieces of paper with carbon

Method:

Do a simple project or play a simple game.

Let each child say something about what you just did, as you write the words. It will look something like this:

We all played tag.
Ken was it.
He tagged Tammy.
She was it.
We ran fast.

Read the story back to the children.

Optional: Using carbon and paper you can make copies for each child to take home.

Trips

VISITING A NEIGHBORHOOD ARTIST   ages 3 and up

Be aware of different crafts and hobbies that people in the neighborhood enjoy—ceramics, photography and developing, gardening, stained glass, painting, weaving, etc.

Method:

Ask a neighbor if he would be willing to let the playgroup watch him work some morning for a short while. Emphasize that you do not expect them to understand the technique of the skill, but rather to gain an appreciation of what others can do.

Suggestion:

A nice way to say "thank you" would be to bake a simple cookie recipe before you go and share a snack with the person you're visiting. This allows for an informal time to ask questions.

Woodworking

MAKING KEY HANGERS OR POTHOLDER HANGERS   ages 4 and up

Materials:

piece of wood per child, ¾ inch thick, any convenient size for hanging keys. (For example, 5"x10", or 9"x6")

6 cup hooks per person (actual number will depend on the board
   size—plan so hooks will be far enough apart so removal of keys is
   easy)
hammer
nails
paint brush
Deft (a quick-drying varnish available at hardware stores)
Elmer's glue
paste brushes
picture hangers on tape
1 picture per child—size of ¼ to ⅓ of the board area

Use:
   1. Pictures or parts of pictures saved from the children's own work.
   2. Pictures you ask the children to bring from home.
   3. Pictures from calendars, greeting cards, etc. Nature pictures are particularly appealing.

Method:
   Ahead of time: Stain or paint the pieces of wood.
   Place nail holes in boards where hooks are to be screwed in.
With the children: Help the children glue their pictures to their boards. Use glue sparingly. Wipe with damp cloth. Allow time to dry. Let them brush the Deft over the whole piece of wood. Help them screw the hooks into the holes. Help them attach the picture hanger to the back side.

MAY

May Contents

May Guideposts

Things You Can Collect

No doubt about it—spring is finally here. Wherever you live—in northern climes or southern—sunshine and comfortable temperatures prevail. You may want to begin collecting a few items in further preparation for the many warm days to come.

BLEACH BOTTLES

Pails and scoops will be in demand for sandbox or mudpie play. They will also be needed for the summer collecting of shells, stones, tadpoles and minnows. These are items frequently lost or left behind, so why not plan to accumulate some bleach bottles for making a few? Alert your friends so they will set aside some plastic bottles for you.

For the pails you will slice off the upper part of the bottle, including the handle. Make a handle by using cord tied through holes punched on opposite sides of the container. A collar cut from the bottle and trimmed to handle shape, then hooked on with paper fasteners works well, as does any type of sturdy plastic strip.

For scoops. leave the existing handle, Holding the bottle on its side, cut a piece diagonally from the bottom of the bottle leaving a generous opening for scooping.

Plan a pail-and-scoop-decorating project. Supply magic markers, crayon, contact paper, glue and felt or any combination of materials that strike your fancy. Ornamenting the toys can be as much fun as the using. Some children may be eager to scamper off and dig right away. That is all right. Later they will remember what materials you suggested for decorating and may try it by themselves. Others will find the art project more absorbing than the digging.

Perhaps someone will even have an original decorating scheme. One artistic child gathered an assortment of leaves and flowers and Scotch-taped them to her pail for a whimsical springlike touch. Of course it was not lasting, but it was completely original and creative.

SEEDS OR SEEDLINGS

Get ready for some earnest gardening projects. Maybe you can save a few seeds from your kitchen. Fruits and vegetables provide the source. If a store visit is easier, choose seed packets there. Check the germination time. Early sprouters such as beans, corn, squash, marigolds or zinnias are most encouraging to watch. Once children plant something, they want near-instant results!

While you are seed shopping, pick up some potting soil. If you have a green thumb, you might enjoy making your own. Dig earth from under trees in the woods; find soil from gardens or vacant lots; gather sand from a creek (seashore sand is too salty). Mix the lot and toss in peat moss for good measure. This combination with the help of a little fertilizer will give the children's plants a good start.

When your preschoolers appear on the scene, equip them with whatever containers you have handy. Egg cartons, dixie cups, tin cans, styrofoam cups or milk cartons are all good. Punch a few holes in the bottom for drainage. The children can spoon soil into the pots and be all ready for planting their seeds or transplanting seedlings (see May activities TRANSPLANTING FUN and GOING TO SEE A NURSERY IN SPRINGTIME).

Take a minute to talk about the care of the plants—water, enough sunlight and proper planting. Make it a point to brief the playgroup adults if they are not familiar with simple gardening techniques.

Remember the Familiar

PLANTS POPPING UP

You may not take time for a full-fledged springtime gardening project with your preschoolers, but if you do have a garden, let the children troop out to search for fresh sprouts. Show them how to walk around the garden's edge and how to gently push aside the leaves to reveal the new shoots of old plants beginning to pop up.

STORIES AND SNACK OUTSIDE

Another way to enjoy the warm lovely days together is to plan normal indoor activities for outside. For example, you can spare yourself the kitchen crumbs. Help your youngsters fill thermoses and sandwich bags with snacks or lunchtime goodies. Hunt for an appealing picnic site by a pond, in a nearby park or under a tree in your own back yard. Make sure you have tucked a storybook or small volume of spring poems into your bag, so you all can share storytelling time while everyone munches the picnic treats.

Later you might continue the outing with a trek to look for window boxes in early bloom, lingering to watch the sweeper clean the streets should he come by—or drinking in any exciting "happening" along the way. City streets, suburban roads or country lanes will offer equally absorbing surprises.

MOTHER'S DAY

Do not forget that May is the month for Mother's Day. Children love to create surprises to show their love. If you think you will not have time for a special project, you can set aside some of the children's work from April, provided, of course, that you have planned ahead. Perhaps you were particularly pleased with their April STORY OF ME. These would make delightful Mother's Day cards. Maybe you can tuck away the MAY DAY BASKETS, KEY HANGERS OR POTHOLDER HANGERS (all from April) to send home closer to Mother's Day.

If you do undertake a new project especially for the occasion, consider the PAPER FLOWER BOUQUET.

Mothers always enjoy photographs of their offspring. You may have taken pictures of the group singly and together. Have one reproduced for each child. Let the youngsters personalize a picture mat with pretty decorations to frame it.

If your preschoolers are about ready for another cut-and-paste activity, let them cut and paste "the reasons why I love you." Snip pictures from magazine pages and glue onto a big heart or placemat for a Mother's Day collage. Cover with clear contact paper to preserve.

The world outside is coming alive. The additional time you spend in the fresh air will give everything you do an added excitement and fresh perspective. Not least, you will notice that it is not just the plants that are growing—the children are too! They are taller, but more importantly they are more mature, have a longer attention span and are *so* much easier to manage! Whether you are tackling a bleach bottle project or searching for sprouts, you will find yourself relaxing more when you are in their presence and looking forward to sharing summer days with them.

May Activities

Arts and Crafts

CLOTHESLINE ART SHOW   ages 3 and up

Materials:
   clothesline (hung low)
   clothespins (clip type)
   variety of artwork done by children (save during year, or have
      children bring a few samples from home)

Method:
   Children help clip art to clothesline.
      Invite willing neighbor, car-pool mother or other guests to view.
   Serve some goody the children have made for snacktime.

Suggestion
   Ask the children what they wish to name each picture. Put the title
   on with magic marker. Make sure the artist's name is on, too!

CLOTHESPIN SAILBOAT   age 4 and up

Materials:
   clip-type clothespins—1 per child
   toothpicks
   white paper—one sheet 9"x12" will do, cut into pices needed
   glue and brushes
   scissors
   optional: magic markers or paint and brushes

Method:
   Ahead of time: Remove metal from clothespins. Draw squares on
   white paper (approximately 2½"x2½"). Make a sample boat of
   your own. (see directions below)
   With the children: Show them your sample. Children glue flat
   parts of clothespins together. This leaves a tiny hole near one end of

the "boat." While glue is drying, children cut the paper squares. You insert a toothpick "mast" through each paper square sail. *(Optional:* Children color the boats.) Then the children put glue in the boat's hole and stand the toothpick mast in it. Let dry.

Variation:
A small amount of clay at the end of the toothpick might be a quicker and more secure way to attach the mast to the clothespin boat.

DRAWING WITH CARBON PAPER   ages 3 and up

Materials:
carbon paper
paper light enough for use with carbon paper
pencils
paper clips

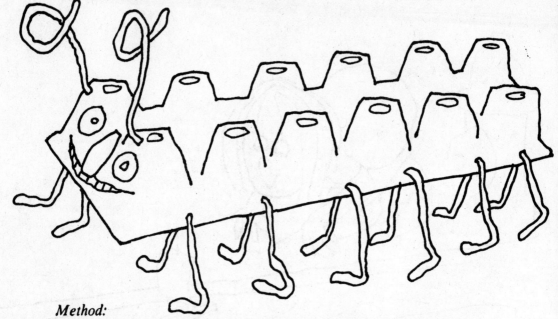

Method:

Clip two pieces of paper with carbon between for each child. Children experiment drawing and lifting the paper to see the identical impressions beneath.

EGG-CARTON BUTTERFLY   ages 3 and up

Materials:

egg cartons divided into 2-4 compartments (depending on desired size of butterfly)

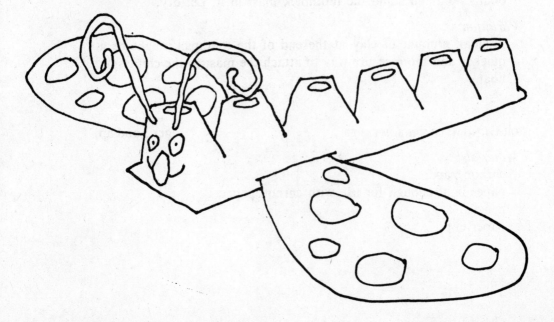

pipe-cleaners—2 (colored ones are most effective)
construction paper wings—2 each
tempera paint and brushes or magic markers
scotch tape or stapler
scissors

Method:
Ahead of time: Divide the egg cartons for the body of the butterfly and cut a pair of wings for each child's butterfly from the construction paper. Mix the paints and store in small jars.
With the children: Let each child select a color to paint his egg-
carton body. Then let them exchange colors to paint the wing
designs. When dry, help assemble the parts with tape or a stapler.

Variations:
1. Another time the children might enjoy making an egg-carton
caterpillar from a carton cut in half vertically. Let them paint the
body solid or with stripes and dots. Attach pipe-cleaner feelers and
make eyes.
2. Ladybugs made from one carton section are fun, too. Or use the
whole carton to create an outer-space creature. Feelers from pipe-
cleaners and painted spots on the carton section will make the
ladybug.
3. For turtles, cut a flat turtle shape from construction paper to
provide the head, legs and tail. Have the children paint the carton
section for the turtle's shell and then glue it to the construction
paper shape.

MAKE A PUZZLE   ages 3 and up

Materials:
1 piece oaktag or cardboard (about 9"x12") per child
crayons
scissors

Method:
Each child creates a picture. Cut the picture into three or four
pieces for a puzzle. Cut in straight lines, not complicated curves. A
child with good cutting ability may cut his own.

Suggestions:
   Game: Sit in a circle. Children put their puzzle pieces in a pile in the middle all mixed up. Then everyone finds his pieces and puts together his own puzzle. Repeat, but each child does someone else's puzzle.

PAPER FLOWER BOUQUET   ages 3 and up

Materials:
   egg carton—cut into single sections with hole punched in bottom of each (2-3 per child)
   tissue-paper circles—2-3 inches diameter—four circles per flower with hole in center of each
   pipe-cleaners
   poster paint
   paint brushes

margarine tubs or small juice cans (decorate with spray paint) oasis, (clay, styrofoam or play dough will do)

Method:

Ahead of time: Using egg carton and/or tissue paper, cut sections, circles and make holes.

With the children: Children paint the egg-carton sections, put pipe-cleaners through holes in sections and/or paper circles to make stems. Twist tissue-paper circles around stems. Tissue will untwist partially to make a flower. Each child will make one or more, depending on capability and interest. They will put oasis or clay into the containers and arrange the flowers by pushing stems into the oasis.

Suggestion:

You may also fashion flower shapes with pipe-cleaners alone.

Cooking

SNACK MIX   ages 3 and up

Materials:

popped popcorn	small pretzel sticks
peanuts	Pepperidge Farm goldfish crackers
raisins	paper cup measure
chocolate bits	individual bowls

Method:

Give the children dixie cups to measure equal amounts of each ingredient desired or available. Then let them mix in bowls with their fingers or a spoon.

Suggestion:

This makes a nice snacktime treat for outside play. You could make it just before a trip to a nearby playground, walk through the woods, or swinging and bike-riding in your own yard.

Dramatic Play

ACTING OUT STORIES AND SONGS   ages 3 and up

Story suggestions:
   Jack and Jill
   Three Little Kittens

The Three Bears
Three Billy Goats Gruff
Millions of Cats
Bundle Book (Krauss)

Song Suggestions:
  I'm a Little Teapot
  Old MacDonald
  London Bridge
  Little Red Caboose
  Sing a Song of Sixpence
  Little Jack Horner

Method:
  Enjoy reading the story or singing the song until it is very familiar
  to everyone. Let the children choose the part or parts they would
  like in the acting and keep rotating until everyone has had a turn to
  try his choices. Let the children use their imagination for simple
  props, facial expression and body motion. The more often this activity is repeated the more creative it becomes.

Suggestions:
  The children may first just do the motions while you read or sing
  the accompaniment. Later let them try to incorporate the speak-
  ing—expressing the idea in their own words.

STYROFOAM PUPPET   ages 3 and up

Materials:
  different-sized styrofoam balls
  popsicle sticks
  common pins
  glue, brushes and Q-tips
  material scraps
    large 11" squares for main clothing (covers child's hand and
      puppet stick)
    small scraps for details
  yarn, ribbon or string
  scissors—pair for each child
  cupcake papers (good for collars or hats)
  magic markers

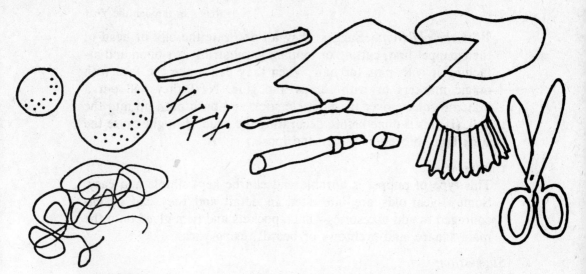

Method:

Ahead of time: Select material scraps interesting in design and texture. Cut the large squares (11" for larger styrofoam balls, smaller squares for the little balls). Sort and spread out the other materials.

With the children: Suggest they all decorate the ball or head of their puppet first, cutting or looping yarn, string or ribbon and attaching it with pins for hair. Then they can make the face with magic markers or with scraps and glue. Next they will put a material square over the popsicle stick and push both up into the ball. (If this is done before decorating the head, it might cause the stick hole to become larger and loose.)

Comment:

This type of puppet is durable and can be kept simple and easy. Some 4-year-olds are interested in detail and they can be encouraged to add accesories—hats, pockets and trim glued onto the main square, and eyebrows or beards, using yarn.

Suggestion:

If pins prove too hazardous to keep in puppets, let child glue features to the puppet and then insert pin to hold while drying. When dry, pull out pin.

Games

SEQUENCE PUZZLE PICTURES   ages 4 and up

Materials:
   old torn storybooks or nursery-rhyme books
   magazines
   scissors
   clear contact paper
      or
   white glue and water (4:1)
   mixing bowl
   spoon
   waxed paper

Method:

Ahead of time: Cut a series of 3-5 pictures that tell familiar stories when placed in sequence. To make these pictures more durable, cover either with clear contact paper or dip in the glue mixture and let dry on the waxed paper for 1 hour; then cover with a 2nd sheet of waxed paper and a heavy book and let press flat overnight.

With the children: Take one story or nursery rhyme and mix the pictures up. Have the children put the pictures back in the right order and tell the story in their own words. Then let them each have a set of pictures and unscramble them to tell a story.

Variations:

1. Another time, mix *all* the story pictures together and see if they can separate them by sets and then rearrange each set to tell the story in sequence.

2. Older children might enjoy hunting through magazines and damaged books for unassociated pictures that just appeal to them and then see if they can create a story sequence all their own.

TELEPHONE GAME   ages 4 and up

Method:

Have the group sit in a circle. The first child thinks of a short sentence or long word and whispers it to the next child until it reaches the end of the line. The last person repeats out loud what he has heard then compares it to what first was said. The result may be very funny. Be sure each child is given a chance to start a message.

Music

LISTENING TO MUSIC—SHOW AND TELL   ages 3 and up

Materials:

record player

a record that tells a story—

Examples:

Red Riding Hood

or

The Three Little Pigs

Method:

Listen to the record. Then talk about the way music was used—the trip through the woods, the wind, the wolf, other descriptive themes.

You might say:

"Let's listen to this part where Red Riding Hood is going through

the woods to Grandma's."
(listen to the part)
"Is it a happy, or a sad, or a scared sound?"
   or
"Listen to the wolf music."
(listen)
"What kind of a sound was that?"

Suggestion:
Let the children take turns telling parts of the story while the others add musical touches. You could have a "kitchen orchestra," homemade, or other instruments handy for them to choose from—bells for Red Riding Hood, drum or pan to beat for the wolf, etc.

Variations:
1. (for 4-year-olds) Listen to two short record versions of the same story. Compare the two.
"In which was the wolf more scary?" "Why?"
"In which was the wind more blowy?" "Why?"
"In which was Red Riding Hood happier sounding?" "Why?"
2. (for 4-year-olds) You could compare the musical sounds of two entirely different stories, listening for happy, sad, mad or scared feelings expressed through music.
3. You and the children make up a story and add musical sound effects with homemade or "kitchen orchestra" instruments.

MUSICAL CHAIRS   ages 3 and up

An old favorite

Materials:
chairs
music (use a record player or clap your hands)

Method:
Chairs are lined up—always one less than the number of children playing. Children move around the chairs, sit down when the music stops, and the one left sits to the side. A chair is removed, then another and yet another until only one child is left.

Physical Exercise

FOLLOW THE LEADER   **ages 3 and up**

Large-muscle coordination

Method:
A child is selected to be leader. Other children line up behind him. The other children copy him in his motions. Then a new leader is picked.

Ideas for Motions:
jump up and down
wheelbarrow—2 children
bounce a ball and walk
skipping
wave arms up and down
somersaults
hopping on one foot
bending at waist and touching toes

Variation:
This is similar to "Simon Says." Both can be adapted to gym skills.

MUSICAL BALL GAME   **ages 3½ and up**

Materials:
ball
record (or you clap)
record player

Method:
Children pass the ball to one another as they stand in a circle. The younger the group, the closer they stand. You stop the music at different points to "catch" someone with the ball. Keep on till everyone has had a chance to be caught.

Science

MINIATURE GREENHOUSE   **ages 3 and up**

Great activity after a trip to a greenhouse!

Materials:
    transparent covered dish (deep enough to allow for growth of
        seedlings) or a clear plastic container with clear plastic wrap held
        by rubber band for cover—1 per child
    gravel or small pebbles for drainage
    garden soil
    spoons
    seeds
    water

Method:
Using spoons or fingers, children cover bottom of dish with gravel
or pebbles: then add layer of soil 1 ¼" or more deep. Sprinkle a few
seeds. Cover with thin layer of soil. Water. *(Be careful not to
flood!)* Cover. Cover will keep moisture in for a long time.
    Children put this in sunny place at home. With help rewater as
needed. Later transplant to pot or garden.

TESTING OUR SENSES—   ages 3 and up
WHAT DO WE SEE, HEAR, FEEL, SMELL

Method:
    The place is *anywhere!* Lie on your tummy. Close your eyes. Talk
    about these one at a time:
        What can we hear?
        What can we feel?
        What can we smell?
    Open your eyes.
        What can we see?

TRANSPLANTING FUN   ages 3 and up

Materials:
    disposable plastic cups (holes punched in bottom for drainage)
        or
    small plant pots—1 per child
    spoons
    trowel
    plants from your garden (something that needs thinning) like your
        phlox, mums, bleeding heart or calendula)

pebbles
optional: ribbon, liquid fertilizer

Method:
Let the children find a few pebbles to put in the bottom of their pots. Spoon a little soil into the cup. Help them each dig up a small plant, showing how to dig wide around the plant and deep enough to get all the roots. Explain that the plant drinks water and takes food from the dirt through the roots. Each child will put his plant in the cup and spoon in extra soil to fill the cup. Show them how to pat down the dirt to prevent large air pockets. Water. Add fertilizer, if desired.
Optional: Tie a ribbon around each.

Suggestion:
1. Send home directions for plant care. "Keep in sunny window or transplant in garden. Water."
2. A great Mother's Day gift!

Storytelling

BUTTON BOOK   ages 4 and up

Materials:
6"x9" cloth pieces cut with pinking shears to the same size
assortment of buttons—varying size and color
needle and thread
scissor—sharp points
felt scraps cut into various shapes

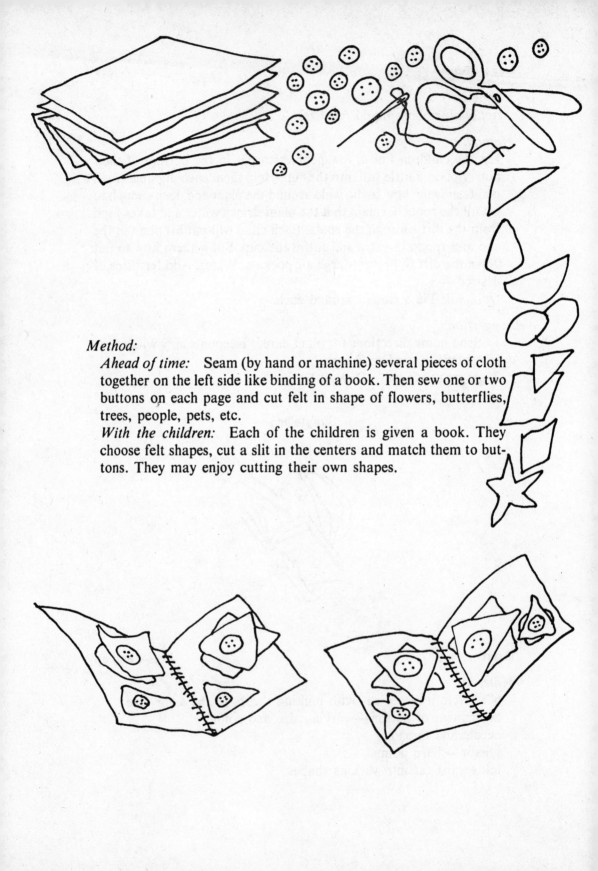

Method:

Ahead of time: Seam (by hand or machine) several pieces of cloth together on the left side like binding of a book. Then sew one or two buttons on each page and cut felt in shape of flowers, butterflies, trees, people, pets, etc.

With the children: Each of the children is given a book. They choose felt shapes, cut a slit in the centers and match them to buttons. They may enjoy cutting their own shapes.

Suggestions:

1. Be sure to leave enough space between buttons so appliques do not overlap.
2. Extra details may be added by gluing on felt or using iron-on tape.

Variations:

1. Gluing buttons on construction paper.
2. Buttoning felt appliques on a large piece of material for a picture—back it with cardboard.

Trips

GOING TO SEE A NURSERY IN SPRINGTIME   ages 3 and up

A large nursery ablaze with springtime color provides the perfect treat for a warm day.

Method:

Your tour can include the seed section, plants in the green houses and flats ready for home planting. Point out where flowers are. Look at the variety of "baby" vegetables and fruits. See whole trees and bushes balled and wrapped, ready to take home. Notice what jobs different workers are doing—plant care, selling. Sample the different fragrances, explore and discover with the children.

Suggestions:

1. This is the perfect time to choose a flat of pretty flowers for the Transplanting Fun activity if you have none to use from your own garden.
    or

2. Take a flat or two home and let the children help you put them in your garden.

VISITING A CARNIVAL OR CIRCUS   ages 3 and up

Plan a trip to watch the circus train unload or go to a nearby neighborhood carnival site and watch the setting-up.

Method:
Plan transportation so that everyone can go in one car. Circus train arrivals are usually very early in the morning—thrilling to see, but maybe difficult to organize for a group at that hour. Neighborhood carnivals usually are set up during the day preceding the opening.
Park at a distance so you will not be in the way.

Look for:

Circus	*Carnival*
different animals	equipment and how it is assembled
how they traveled	carnival games
what they eat	how carnival workers traveled
unusual performers	where food is cooked
(midget, tall man, fat lady)	
where they live between	
performances	
where they get dressed	

Some children will be more interested than others in the mechanics of setting up. If the day is nice, take along a blanket and snack.

Woodworking

FILING   ages 3 and up

This activity generates all sorts of excitement. "Look at the pile of sawdust!" "See the wood getting smaller and smaller!"

Materials:
file—fairly coarse (10" combination shoe rasp is very good)
scrap wood
vise or C-clamp

Method:

Demonstrate the use of the file. Let the children take turns experimenting.

DRILLING   ages 4 and up

Materials:

eggbeater-type drill
scrap wood—thin pieces requiring minimum drilling before the breakthrough
vise or C-clamp

Method:

Put wood in the vise and show how to drill. Let the children take turns experimenting. Encourage them not to turn the handle too quickly and to bear down slightly, putting pressure on the drill.

Comments:

The drill is somewhat unwieldy. Well-coordinated 4 year-olds will manage very well. Others may just enjoy a few tries.

Suggestion:

1. By now the children have had experience with several woodworking skills. Each can operate a different tool while awaiting his turn at the latest addition.
2. Have a supply of cord handy for the drilling activity. Children love to put cord through the holes they make in one piece. They also enjoy stringing and tying pieces together.

BUILDING AND FLOATING BARGES AND BOATS   ages 4 and up

Materials:

scrap lumber
nail assortment
wire scraps
glue
white sheeting or paper
set tubs or a plastic baby tub filled with water

Method:

Suggest the children create some kind of boat. Distribute materials and let them enjoy building; then let them play with their results in the water.

Comments:

Some children may go as far as to partition off the sections of the ferryboat and line up matchbox cars for the crossing. Small plastic figures make good passengers.

JUNE   JULY   AUGUST

June, July and August Contents

June, July and August Guideposts

Things You Can Collect

Summer brings a new dimension to your playgroup arrangements. The warm vacation months offer a different set of circumstances. You will be planning around your family's summer schedules and trips. You may continue to have playgroup regularly, or perhaps you will decide to have a few get-togethers with parents and children instead. Either way, time and location can be more flexible, the day less structured and a fresh spirit of fun added to the playing because of the wealth of outdoor activities possible in the summertime. An added bonus will be the children's comfortable camaraderie which has developed over the months of getting to know one another well.

If your group does not meet during the summer months try some of the suggested activities with your own family. Outdoor walks and "treasure" hunts are pursuits enjoyed by all ages. Whatever form your outings take, accumulate a few items along the way for a head-start on materials and ideas for your next playgroup year. Why not save postcards received or purchased on summer travels? A September storytelling activity about vacations could feature a postcard-movie about summer trips. The children can make the movie by taping together the postcards and then view by running the "film" through slits in a box.

BEACH TREASURES

The prospect of hunting for sea treasures is met with a fever of excitement no matter how frequently the participants have done the same thing. On the last beach trip of the season children will bring back the same full pail with the same enthusiasm for the favorite lucky stone, sand dollar, egg case, seagull feather or sand-smoothed beach glass.

Your hunt may take the form of a game with a specific list of items to look for if the children are familiar enough with the names of beach objects—perfect for a summer birthday party at the beach, too.

The collection may be the inspiration for any number of creative projects. Someone may want to use dried specimens to decorate a block of wood, can or box cover. An accumulation of small smooth stones and a little glue may inspire the creation of whimsical stone animals. A mobile may be the result of discovering a perfect sized piece of driftwood and several particularly lovely shells.

Extra scallop and clam shells could serve as appealing dishes for holding glue. Set aside some extras to add a summer feeling to winter cut-and-paste projects. Making SAND CASTINGS is well worth the effort if you have a variety of dried and "descented" sea creatures and shells. Sand dollars, baby horseshoe crabs, starfish and snail shells make interesting designs.

You and the children might enjoy remembering a cousin or friend who lives in a beachless area. Special prizes culled from the shore, cleaned and coated with a little shellac or clear plastic spray for shine, can be prettily wrapped and sent as surprise gifts.

FLOWERS TO PRESS

Summer does not necessarily mean the seashore to everyone. Discoveries for some groups may center around the field or roadside where there is a profusion of wild flowers. Treasures in this case may be armfuls of daisies or other blossoms to be put in BROWN BOTTLE VASES (see summer activities), paper drinking cups or juice cans for transporting home. A selection of blooms might be saved and pressed in an extra thick book to use later in projects. They may be used to adorn note paper or placemats and covered with clear contact paper for permanent preservation.

Remember the fun of out-of-season materials. On a cold wintry day it might be entertaining to create a special arrangement on paper with pressed flowers and some of the "baby leaves" you set aside in May, so save some for a frigid weather pick-me-up project.

POPSICLE STICKS AND EMPTY ICE CREAM CUPS

There are few places where the ice-cream man is not a part of the summer scene. His popsicles become worth the price (almost) if you save the sticks. Let the children stain, paint or crayon them and use them in any of a hundred ways. Glue around the sides of juice cans for pencil holders; attach to old greeting cards for puppets; wind with yarn to make shade pulls or window decorations; glue crisscross in a square and decorate for hot pads. You can even use them for making your *own* popsicles!

Dixie cups are another ice-cream-man bonus. They are versatile enough for mixing paint, planting seeds or storing paper clips and fasteners.

Remember the Familiar

Repeating favorite warm-weather pastimes from year to year is part of what makes summer such fun. Your family may look forward to long car trips complete with maps and restaurant stops. Maybe fishing and mountain-climbing comprise your summer magic. The ocean or a mudhole at grandpa's farm, the ice-cream man's nightly neighborhood stop, regular trips to a nearby frog pond—any or all may constitute what makes summer an adventure for you. Think of what some of your old favorites are, and then share one or two with your playgroup. You may be introducing the youngsters to a completely new experience.

SAFETY

Whatever your plans are, make safety a part of them. Spend time with the children going over rules for safe fun in the water, on a bicycle, and hiking. You might play "pretend" and help the children act out some summer problem situations—like what to do if you are lost in the woods or in a crowd, or how to seek help quickly if a friend is having trouble in the water. It would not hurt for you to review some simple first aid procedures so you will be better prepared should an emergency arise.

FATHER'S DAY

One of the first celebrations of the summer months is Father's Day. Gifts made with love mean so much. Let the children have a real part in deciding what gift to give. Thinking of something to please their dads will teach them that part of the fun of giving is the planning and anticipating.

The present can be something as simple as a painting mounted on construction paper or the WOODEN RULER made especially with Father's office or workshop in mind.

Daddies enjoy photographs just as mothers do. Perhaps you could use pictures of the children as part of a MEMORY TRAY gift (see February), or let each child create a decorative border on a piece of construction paper and simply mount a single photograph on it.

The preschoolers could plan a special culinary treat for Dad—decorated cookies, PEANUT-CORN CRUNCH (September) or BONBONS (April) are a few simple tasty ideas from which you can choose. How about writing special invitations for a walk or bike ride with Dad. Hook it to or print it right on the bagged goodies. Daddy and his little one can enjoy the snack while they are off on their special outing together.

FOURTH OF JULY

The Fourth of July is the most exciting of summer celebrations. The children will be eagerly anticipating parades, picnics and fireworks displays, so you will be talking about it before the actual day.

Let the children make their own "fireworks" with STRAW PAINTING. Many children love making loud, explosive noises as they blow and spread the paint.

For a holiday craft project. Make "firecrackers" from toilet-tissue tubes or other cardboard tubes cut to five or six inches. Tape heavy construction paper to seal the bottom shut. The children glue on a covering of red paper (precut to size by you) and decorate with gold stars and flag stickers. You precut circles of construction paper with the same circumference as that of the tube. Put a hole in the center. Insert a few inches of string and tape firmly on one side for a firecracker "wick". Use tape to hook the circle hinge-fashion to the open end of the tube. What a delightful firecracker, and it can double as a candy holder, too!

The children may have a spontaneous parade—or you can all plan one complete with rhythm band instruments, flags and wagons or trikes decorated in red, white and blue trappings. Choose a route down the street or around the block to show off your parade.

If weather permits, let lunchtime be a hot-dog cookout on the grill. You can make the party as elaborate or simple as you please. Include

a game or two. Four-year-olds love to try potato-sack racing—non-competitively of course. Old pillowcases can substitute for sacks and the activity is one that can be done inside with equal success.

SNOWBALLS

Remember how you tried some spring style treats to make mid-winter seem less dreary? Pull a similar switch on a steaming hot day. If you tucked some snowballs into your freezer last January, pull them out for cooling punch or have a snowball "toss" using a tree as a target. The group might just enjoy watching how the sun will melt a snowball—in a little pail of water or on the hot sidewalk.

Catch the spirit of colder weather by beating soapflakes to make winter snow pictures or sculptures (see February—WHIPPING SNOW).

Summer never is long enough. Somehow you just cannot fit in all the activities that you dreamt of doing during warm weather. Certainly this is true with planning for your little group. You cannot possibly squeeze in everything that seems appealing from the search for beach treasures to the snowball "toss." Be selective—then savor what you choose. You will have lots of happy memories to warm the colder days ahead.

June, July and August
Activities

Arts and Crafts

BROWN BOTTLE VASE   ages 3 and up

Materials:
  brown bottle or jar (such as Coffeemate jar) 1 per child
  sand
  glue and brushes
  large pan lined with waxed paper

Method:
  Put sand into paper-lined pan. Children brush glue all over their
  jars; roll jar in sand.

Suggestion:
  Let children pick a few flowers to take home in their vases. Wild
  flowers and weed flowers from a field are particularly lovely in this
  vase.

DECORATED SEASHELLS OR STONES   ages 3 and up

Materials:
  shells—medium sized clam, scallop or other shell to use as base
  assorted tiny shells, starfish—or stones
  other tiny ornaments that would look well with shells such as:
    colored crushed glass, small pearls, tiny plastic seahorses
  glue and brushes
  Note:
  Most of these materials are available at hobby shops if you have not
  had access to a beach.

Method:
  Children decorate the medium-sized shells or stones by gluing on
  smaller ornaments and shells.

FOURTH OF JULY STRAW PAINTING   ages 4 and up

Materials:
    poster paint—3-4 bright colors
    straws
    paper—12"x18"—1 per child
    cover-ups—smocks, old shirts, etc.

Method:
    DO OUTDOORS! Pour pools of paint into the center of the paper.
    Children spread paint by blowing with straw or by using tip of straw
    as a paintbrush.

PAINTING WITH WATER   ages 3 and up

Baby brothers and sisters can easily join in.

Materials:
    large paint brushes (Daddy's will be great)
    pails or cans of water

Method:
    Children can "paint" the house, garage, car, or sidewalk. This ac-
    tivity might not sound exciting but it is delightful in hot weather,
    and its simplicity absolutely consumes small children.

SHADOW BOX SHELLS   ages 4 and up

Materials:
    shoebox covers or any box cover about that depth
    scissors
    scotch tape
    clear plastic wrap

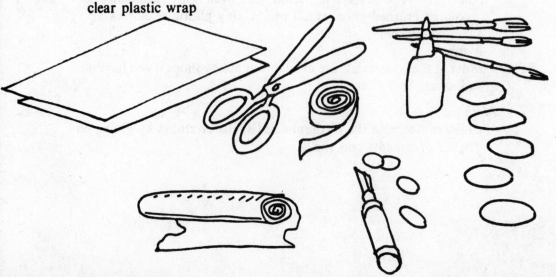

glue and brushes
magic marker
optional: colored paper or paint (paper is tidier; poster paint
spreads when children glue objects to it)

Method:
Children may want to paint their boxes first or glue in background
paper. After the paint dries, have the children glue shells inside to
make butterflies, birds, flowers, etc. They put in details with magic
markers (antennae, designs on wings, stems). Then stretch clear
wrap around boxes to make a "glass front" and help children tape it
securely on the back.

Suggestions:
Clam or mussel shells side by side make good butterflies. Tiny
clam, scallop or jingle shells make good flower petals or leaves.

Variation:
Older children—perhaps big brothers and sisters—working at the
same time might enjoy the project of making their own box from
oaktag or construction paper.
Method: Cut oaktag to desired size for shadow box (about 5" by 7"
is good). Fold all edges over ½" to ¾". Cut as indicated on the
dark lines (see sketch). Bend up sides ready for children to tape tag
ends over so that the box shape holds. Continue as above.

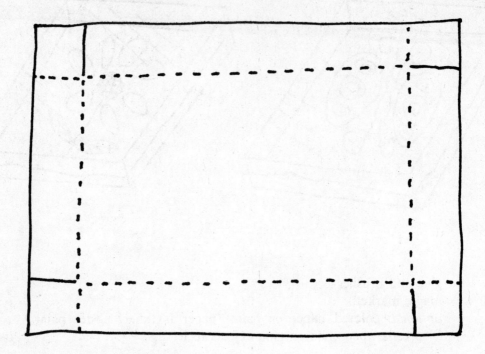

A CHILD'S AMERICAN FLAG   ages 3 and up

Materials:
1 piece each of red, white, and blue paper per child at least 5"x7"
gold star stickers or a smaller piece of white paper for making stars
paste or glue and brushes
a small American flag, a picture of one, or a sample one made
    ahead of time by you

Method:
Show the children the American Flag and ask what shapes and
colors they see in it—blue rectangle, red lines, stripes. Distribute
paper and encourage children to tear red stripes and a blue piece to
paste onto the larger white piece. Some children may wish to tear a
few white pieces to glue onto the blue as stars, or one or more
sticker stars may be used. Numbers of stripes or stars and accuracy
do not matter.

Comment:
This project is particularly good for groups who find cutting difficult.

SAND CASTINGS   **Ages 4 and up**

Materials:
   foil or tin pan of any shape—must be as deep as the largest shell
   damp sand
   Red Top (a quick plaster of paris)
   large can and stick for mixing plaster
   fish line and scissors or heavy string
   variety of dried and "descented" sea creatures and/or shells
      examples: starfish, sand dollars, crab and snail shells, clam and
      scallop shells

Method:
   Ahead of time: This activity is best done outdoors at a picnic table
   or in the kitchen or basement. Set out all the materials in large
   buckets and even have the amount of water ready for mixing the
   Red Top according to package directions. This takes a fair amount
   of plaster of paris, so you would need to use at least a five-pound
   bag.
   With the children: Have them line each pan with damp sand like a
   thick pie crust, using their hands to pat it down evenly. Then show
   them how to push the shells into the sand until they are approximately level with the top of the sand "crust" (remember that
   the part pushed down first and covered by the sand will be what
   shows when it has hardened and the tin is removed). When everyone
   is happy with their shell arrangements, mix the plaster, allowing
   them to help stir. Then *quickly* pour the white mixture into the
   remaining space—like pie filling. Immediately help insert both ends
   of a fish line or heavy string into the plaster so it will be ready to
   hang when dry. You might also take a stick and mark the date or
   child's name in the plaster.
      Even on a very sunny, warm day it is best to let the sandcasting
   dry and harden in the pan for at least 12 hours. Then the children
   remove the pan and (outside or over a wastebasket) brush away the
   excess sand. The result is a most attractive wall plaque with a thin
   coating of sand covering the plaster and a shell design in relief—a
   wonderful way to preserve a special beach collection.

Cooking

BLUEBERRY JAM   ages 4 and up

A Certo recipe—inexpensive and easy for the children to make

Materials:
  potato masher
  baby food jars or other small sizes, sterilized
  decorated jar covers (spray paint or cover with aluminum foil)
  ladle and metal spoon
  large cooking pot
  paraffin and small melting pot (coffee can will do)
  Recipe ingredients:
  $1^1/2$ qt. ripe blueberries (maybe the children can pick their own)
  2 T. lemon juice
  7 c. sugar (3 lbs.)
  1 bottle Certo

Method:
Wash and crush the berries. Measure $4^1/2$ cups into a very large saucepan. Squeeze the juice from 1 medium-sized lemon (or use bottled juice) and measure 2 T. into the saucepan with the blueberries. Add the 7 cups of sugar. Let the children all stir to mix well. Then boil hard 1 minute on the stove, stirring constantly. Remove from heat and stir in the Certo. Skim off foam with a metal spoon. Since it needs to cool for about 5 minutes to prevent fruit from settling at the top, let the children take turns stirring and skimming for 5 minutes. Ladle into the sterilized jars and cover immediately with $1/8$" hot paraffin.

FANCY ICE CUBES   ages 3 and up

Materials:
  individual Jell-o molds
    or
  ice-cube trays
  fruit juice
    and/or
  water
  small pitcher
  colorful fruits—cherries, pineapple chunks, strawberries, peach
    slices, etc

For serving:
    cups
    pitcher, mixing bowl, or punchbowl
        and
    soup ladle

Method:

Let the children spoon fruits into the molds or cube sections. Let each pour juice over the fruit. They can take turns helping to fill the one or two ice-cube trays if you are using these instead of molds. Freeze.

Put molded ice into bowl and add fruit juice or other drink; or put cubes in cups. Ladle or pour drink into cups. The children can help with all of these steps.

Variation:

Make popsicles instead using fruit juice in tupperware molds or paper cups with recycled popsicle sticks stuck in the center. Place on tray and freeze thoroughly.

ICE CREAM CONE CLOWNS   ages 3 and up

Materials:

ice cream balls (scooped ahead of time and ready in the freezer)
cones
assortment of maraschino cherries, chocolate bits, cut-up gum-
    drops, nut pieces, cut-up fruits and peels
colored paper baking cups

Method:

Children place cup upside down and flatten it on a dish. Sit ice cream ball "head" on top. Place cone "hat" upside down on ice cream. Make eyes, nose, and mouth with assorted edible bits.

Variations:

Ice cream ball set on square of cake; add eyes, nose, mouth with bits; place candle on the top—this can be a jack-o-lantern (using orange sherbet) for Halloween. Replace candles with bunny ears to create a gay Easter bunny.

LEMON SHERBET   ages 3 and up

Easy to make, but give it plenty of freezer time before eating.

Materials:
   empty ice-cube trays or other low flat containers suitable for freez-
   ing sherbet
   mixing bowl
   large spoon
Recipe:
   1 lemon, juice and fine-grated rind
   1 c. granulated sugar
   1 c. whole milk

Method:
   Stir the ingredients well and pour into ice-cube trays and place in
   the freezer. Delicious on a hot day.

Variation: Orange Sherbet
   substitute 1 orange for 1 lemon

SUMMER DRINKS   ages 3 and up

Materials:
   ice cream or sherbet
   spoon or scoop
   paper or plastic cups
   ginger ale/fruit juice combination
   pitcher

Method:
   Put scoop of ice cream in cups and let children pour their own
   drinks.
      Let the children think up names for their drinks and for other
   drink combinations, such as "cranberry-ale" or "ginger-grape."

Dramatic Play

PRETEND BOX   ages as noted

Children enjoy a chance to "make believe"

Materials:
   large box containing props and dress-ups sorted according to role-
      playing such as:

doctor-nurse (3-4 yr. old)
hairdresser-barber (3-4 yr. old)
car mechanic-gas station attendant (4 yr. old)
ballet dancer (4 yr. old)
astronauts (4 yr. old)
chefs-waitresses (4 yr. old)
plumber (4 yr. old)
dentist (4 yr. old)
postman (3-4 yr. old)
mother-father (3-4 yr. old)
policemen and policewomen (3-4 yr. old)
pilot-flight attendant-passenger (3-4 yr. old)

Method:

When the children use the pretend box it is best to choose props for a familiar role. Spend time with them going over each article in the box and hearing their ideas on how members of the group could have a part in using them. After listening to their ideas open the box and let them act out the role on their own. Encourage *both* boys and girls to be doctors, nurses, astronauts, etc.

Variations:

1. Another time ask them about other roles, for example, hairdresser and barber. Hear about their experiences, *then* open the box and let them discover the appropriate props and act out the roles.

2. Read a story and then bring out appropriate props for dramatic play. For example, nurse and doctor props can follow a story about a trip to the hospital—or read a cowboy story before pulling out a box full of western props.

3. A playgroup child's recent experience on an airline might lead mother to put in airline "badges" and other assorted airline souvenirs. A big empty box could be brought out to be the airplane.

PUPPET PAIRS   ages 4 and up

Materials:

socks and/or mittens (matching or unmatching, outgrown or worn out)

glue and brushes
felt scraps
scissors
buttons
darning needle and yarn
magic marker
felt and other materials for making features

Method:
The children can be fairly independent again in making these puppets except for sewing on buttons. The trick, of course, is sewing only through one layer so their hands will still fit way inside. You will need to help here. Encourage them to make a pair and then listen for the interesting conversations they have betweeen their two hands or two feet.

Suggestions:
Handmade puppets are fun. Keep a supply available for tree play. Some mittens are knitted and sold as puppets and could be added to your collection along with any ready-made puppets you have.

With a variety of sock and mitten puppets there can be new fun with Musical Hands and Feet (March activity).

Games

BLOWING BUBBLES   ages 3 and up

Materials:
assortment of bubble wands and pipes

liquid dishwashing soap
water
plastic containers or pans

Method:
Ahead of time: Mix soap and water in plastic containers to make a good bubble-blowing consistency—about ½ water to ½ soap.
With the children: Make bubbles!—outdoors for fewer clean-up problems.

Note:
Straws for blowing bubbles *do* work, but very young children forget and suck in instead of blowing out, gagging and sputtering in the process. The use of pipes tends to alleviate this problem.

HOT POTATO GAME   ages 3 and up

Materials:
small ball
signal—whistle or record and record player

Method:
Have your group sit on the floor in a circle. Roll a ball from one to another as fast as possible so you won't get caught when a signal is given to stop.

INDOOR GAMES OUTDOORS   ages 3 and up

Transfer outdoors some of the indoor games you did during the winter. They will take on a whole new dimension!

Just being outdoors with or without assorted play equipment automatically means running and exercise to children. Enjoy!

Music

A KITCHEN ORCHESTRA   ages 3 and up

Learning to listen to musical patterns made from melodies that are the same or different

Materials:
    pans, pots
    wooden and metal spoons (to use as drumstricks)
    cardboard containers
    plastic containers
    heavy glasses or bottles

Song:
    Hot Cross Buns
    Hot Cross Buns
    One-a-penny, two-a-penny,
    Hot Cross Buns

Method:
    Sing or say the familiar *Hot Cross Buns.* Have the children raise
    their hands on the line where the melody and words change (one-a-
    penny). Repeat, letting the children sing or chant with you and raise
    their hands again at "one-a-penny."
    Let everyone choose an "instrument" from the kitchen supply.
    Divide the group. Part will accompany the "hot cross buns" lines in
    the melody. The other group will play during "one-a-penny, two-a-
    penny."

Variations:
    1. If the children enjoy the activity, expand the understanding by
    letting them make up different ways of moving for the two different
    parts of the song.
    2. Later they might try the same "orchestra" technique with the
    different parts of *Are You Sleeping?* (*Frere Jacques*).
    3. Records with one melody repeated frequently would be pleasant
    background music and good listening practice during some other
    activity.

MUSICAL ART   ages 3 and up

Materials:
    large sheets of newspaper
    crayons
    record—perhaps a lively collection of short nursery rhymes
    record player

Method:

Spread out newspaper on the kitchen floor. Give each child one crayon. Play the record, changing the song at one-or two-minute intervals. Every time the song is changed, have the children exchange colors with one another. Children draw in rhythm to the music.

Variations:

1. Divide the paper into four large sections and let each child use his four sections for four different tunes.
2. Do the original activity but alternate loud and soft, fast and slow music.

RUBBER-BAND GUITAR   ages 3 and up

Materials:

sturdy, low-sided box
rubber bands of different lengths and widths

Method:

Have the children stretch a variety of the rubber bands over their boxes. Let them strum and experiment with the different sounds made.

Suggestion:

Select a familiar strumming song such as *I've Been Working on the Railroad.* Let them take turns accompanying a recording while the others listen, accompanying the group while they sing.

Physical Exercise

BALL-KICKING PRACTICE   ages 3 and up

Materials:

large ball—more than one if available

Method:

Partners are chosen. One partner faces another. They kick the ball back and forth. Gradually widen the distance between partners as the game goes on.

Variation:

Teams can face one another and do the same.

BALLOON VOLLEYBALL   **ages 4 and up**

Materials:

string (tie taut at child-level to make a "pretend" net)
balloons

Method:

Half the group on either side of the "net" bats or throws the balloon across to one another

Science

MAKING COLLECTIONS   **ages 3 and up**

Materials:

box bottom or lid—1 per child
glue and brushes
tape
collection—stones, shells, feathers, a variety such as feather, empty
     bird's egg, twigs from bird's nest, or totally unrelated items

Method:

After a "treasure-hunt" walk in the place of your choice, children glue or tape their treasures into the box bottom or lid. Cover the box with clear wrap and tape to make a "glass" front for viewing. Some children may put in only one or two items.

Variation:

Let them paint and decorate empty cigar boxes to use for collecting summer treasures. This way they are free to handle, sort and periodically inspect or swap their findings.

EXPLORE THE NEIGHBORHOOD—NATURE   ages 3 and up

Materials:

bags or buckets for each child for collecting

Method:

Take a walk.

Look for:

leaves	cultivated flowers
trees	seeds
shrubs	weeds
wildflowers	insects
birds	squirrels
bird's nests	cocoons
animal tracks	mosses

These can be found at private homes, in public parks, on city streets, as well as in the country.

Talk about:

What a weed is.

The difference between a wildflower and one grown in someone's garden.

How leaves have different shapes.

Other facts about the things around you.

Let the discussion grow from what the children discover. For this age group, two or three discoveries and the barest observations about these are plenty to expect in one nature walk.

WHAT PARTS OF A PLANT DO WE EAT?   ages 3 and up

Materials:
a selection of fresh fruits and vegetables chosen from one of the groups below

root	*stem*	*leaves*
carrot	celery	cabbage
radish	asparagus	lettuce
onion		endive
potato		

fruits	*seeds*	*flower*
apple	beans	cauliflower
pear	wheat	broccoli
orange	corn	

There are many more examples for each group which you may think of.

Method:
Choose from one group.
Set the selection on the table.
1. Talk about: where this part of the plant grows (under the ground, on a branch, etc.)
2. Use the terms "root," "stem," "leaf," "fruit," etc.
3. Let the children use the terms themselves.
4. Let answers come from the children wherever possible.
5. Discuss how their own mothers prepare these foods.
6. Let everyone sample the produce.

Suggestions:
1. Precede the activity with a trip to a farm, produce stand or back yard garden to see how the plants look as they grow or when they have just been harvested. Best of all, arrange for the children to harvest their own samples.
2. After sampling from one of the groups listed above, let the children plant their own in small containers to take home with instructions for care (sunny place, watering). Examples: radishes from seed, a carrot from a carrot top.

3. Include a more exotic fruit or vegetable such as a pomegranate, avocado or artichoke.

4. Pictures of plants growing may be used. Possible sources are seed catalogues and library books.

5. Another day, choose one or two more food groups to discuss and sample.

Storytelling

CREATIVE MOVEMENT STORIES   ages 3 and up

Music and drama make the stories

Materials:

Collect an assortment of

1. short, familiar stories or songs appealing to your group
examples:

Three Billy Goats Gruff
Red Riding Hood
Caps for Sale
Ask Mr. Bear
I'm a Little Teapot

2. ideas for experience stories
examples:

     walk in the rain
     planting a garden
     visit to a friend's
     cat and mouse
     first swim of summer
3. records or piano music to accompany

Method:

Experience stories are perhaps best to begin with because the children can develop their own movement to the story and no interaction is needed. First talk about the story and how you can interpret it through body motions. If you are singing a song, go over the words together.

Let's take the garden-planting story. Perhaps you could use the *Romper Room* music for Bend and Stretch or let the children hum familiar tunes as they move around (at this age they often find it difficult to dance and sing at the same time). Talk about how the garden must be hoed, raked, holes made for the seeds and then carefully covered with earth. Last of all you will water the garden. Listen to the music and think about your movements. Then put the story together. Encourage a variety of interpretations by the children as they become more at home with this kind of story.

Trips

TRIP TO YOUR FAVORITE SWIMMING PLACE   **ages 3 and up**

Every family has its favorite swimming place, whether it is a nearby "swimming hole", the community pool, the beach or some other appealing spot. Share it with your playgroup.

Method:

Ahead of time: Let the other parents know what their children will need to bring—swimsuits, towel, picnic lunch, etc. Arrange for another mother or friend to join you as an extra pair of eyes to insure the children's safety in the water.

With the children. Let your group know what the "rules for the day" are: what their boundaries are, a "buddy" system, and anything else that comes to mind for making the day happier and safer. Then have a wonderful time!

Suggestions:

1. If you are at the beach, have a shell and stone "treasure hunt." Arm the children with pails and set off along the shoreline to collect. You might make a list of eight or ten items (drift wood, seaweed, clamshells and so on) and see who can find all of them first.

2. If it is a rainy day be prepared with alternate plans.

3. Don't forget the many other summertime outings that can be shared with your group—for example: wild blueberry picking, a boat ride, or an amusement park treat.

4. Remember the availability of teenage sitters this time of the year. You might welcome the extra help provided by an enthusiastic teenager on one of your summer outings. The children will enjoy it too.

VISITING A MARSH, POND, OR STREAM   ages 4 and up

Materials:

pails or plastic bottles

strainers and/or a net

magnifying glass

optional: a well-illustrated paperback book on marsh, pond or stream life

a knife or scissors for snipping samples

Method:

Supply each child with a container. Ask the children to see what discoveries they can make.

Look for:	*Where to look:*
plants	the water's surface
animals	under the water
mineral objects	at the waters edge
(stones, etc.)	under rocks
	amidst waterside growth
	some yards away from the water
	in bushes and trees

What you might find:

algae	fish	birds
waterbugs	newts	water lilies
tadpoles	salamanders	iris
frogs	insects	cattails
turtles	water plants	etc.

Look at small discoveries under the magnifying glass. Let the children collect some of their finds for taking home. Use the strainers for scooping creatures and plants from the water. Help the children identify what they have found. Let them tell what they already know about it. You may add a fact or two.

Suggestions:

1. Remember that you are not giving a college course in biology The experience of looking closely at the surroundings is the important thing. A deluge of facts is unnecessary.

2. Help the children learn to respect the environment. Avoid littering. Obey rules that may be in effect regarding picking plants. It is forbidden in some areas. If you take a creature such as a frog or turtle home, let the children know he is happier in his own environment and that you plan to return him to it.

Woodworking

WOODEN RULER—A GIFT FOR DADDY   ages 3 and up

Materials:

yardsticks—1 per child. These can be obtained free or at low cost from the lumber yard or hardware store.

vise or C-clamp
saw
sandpaper

Method:
Draw a line between 12 ½" and 13" on the yardstick. Let each child
put the yardstick in the vise and saw down the line. He may then
sandpaper the rough end. He takes the piece he has sawed off home
to Daddy to use as a ruler on his desk.

Suggestions:
1. Take time to talk about how rulers and yardsticks are used.
2. If a special occasion such as Father's Day is coming up, make
the gift special by supplying wrapping materials for the children.

Appendix 1

Nursery Rhymes, Rounds, and Other Familiar Songs

NURSERY RHYMES

Baa Baa Black Sheep

Baa, Baa, Black Sheep,
Have you any wool?
Yes sir, yes sir,
Three bags full;
One for my master,
One for my dame,
But none for the little boy
Who cries in the lane.

Farmer in the Dell

The farmer in the dell,
The farmer in the dell,
Heigh-o the derry-o,
The farmer in the dell.

Repeat, using:
The farmer takes a wife
The wife takes a child
The child takes a nurse
The nurse takes a dog
The dog takes a cat
The cat takes a rat
The rat takes the cheese
The cheese stands alone

Here We Go 'Round The Mulberry Bush

Here we go 'round the mulberry bush,
The mulberry bush, the mulberry bush;
Here we go 'round the mulberry bush,
So early in the morning.

Mon.　This is the way we wash our clothes,
　　　Wash our clothes, wash our clothes;

This is the way we wash our clothes,
So early on Monday morning.

Repeat, using:
Tues.—iron our clothes
Wed.—scrub the floors
Thurs.—sew our clothes
Fri.—sweep the house
Sat.—bake our bread.
Sun.—go to church

Hickory Dickory Dock

Hickory, dickory, dock;
The mouse ran up the clock;
The clock struck one,
The mouse ran down;
Hickory, dickory, dock.

Hot Cross Buns

Hot cross buns,
Hot cross buns;
One a penny, two a penny,
Hot cross buns.

Teensy Weensy Spider

The teensy weensy spider
Crawled up the water spout
Down came the rain and washed the spider out
Out came the sun and dried up all the rain
So the teensy weensy spider climbed up the spout again.

Jack and Jill

Jack and Jill went up the hill
To fetch a pail of water;
Jack fell down
And broke his crown,
And Jill came tumbling after.

Little Jack Horner

Little Jack Horner sat in a corner,
Eating a Christmas pie;
He put in his thumb, and pulled out a plum,
And said, "What a good boy am I!"

Little Miss Muffet

Little Miss Muffet sat on a tuffet,
Eating some curds and whey;
There came a great spider,
And sat down beside her,
And frightened Miss Muffet away.

London Bridge

London Bridge is falling down,
Falling down, falling down,
London Bridge is falling down,
My fair lady.

Mary Had a Little Lamb

Mary had a little lamb,
Little lamb, little lamb,
Mary had a little lamb,
Its fleece was white as snow.

And everywhere that Mary went,
Mary went, Mary went,
And everywhere that Mary went,
The lamb was sure to go.

It followed her to school one day,
School one day, school one day,
It followed her to school one day,
Which was against the rule.

So the teacher turned him out,
But still he lingered near,
And waited patiently about,
Till Mary did appear.

Old King Cole

Old King Cole
Was a merry old soul,
And a merry old soul was he.
He called for his pipe
And he called for his bowl
And he called for his fiddlers three.

Pop Goes the Weasel

All around the cobbler's bench
The monkey chased the weasel;
The monkey tho't t'was all in fun,
Pop! goes the weasel.

Ring Around the Rosie

Ring around the rosie,
Pocket full of posies
Ashes, ashes
We all fall down.

Rock-A-Bye Baby

Rock-a-bye, baby, in the tree top,
When the wind blows, the cradle will rock;
When the bough breaks, the cradle will fall,
And down will come baby, cradle and all.

Rain, Rain Go Away

Rain, rain, go away
Come again another day.
Little (*name of child*) wants to play.
Rain, rain, go away.

Do You Know the Muffin Man

Oh, do you know the muffin-man,
the muffin-man, the muffin-man?
Do you know the muffin-man
Who lives down Drury Lane?

Yes, I know the muffin-man,
the muffin-man, the muffin-man.

Yes 1 know the muffin-man
Who lives down Drury Lane.

Old MacDonald Had a Farm

Old MacDonald had a farm,
Ee-igh, ee-igh, oh.
And on that farm he had some (chicks).
Ee-igh, ee-igh, oh.

Chorus:
With a (chick, chick) here
And a (chick, chick) there.
Here a (chick).
There a (chick).
Everywhere a (chick, chick).

Repeat, using:
duck—quack
turkey—gobble
pig—oink
cow—moo
donkey—hee-haw

Humpty Dumpty

Humpty Dumpty sat on a wall,
Humpty Dumpty had a great fall.
All the king's horses
And all the king's men
Couldn't put Humpty together again.

Twinkle, Twinkle, Little Star

Twinkle, twinkle, little star,
How I wonder what you are!
Up above the world so high,
Like a diamond in the sky.

See-saw, Margery Daw

See-saw Margery Daw,
Jacky shall have a new master;
Jacky must have but a penny a day,
Because he can't work any faster.

ROUNDS

Three blind mice, three blind mice,
See how they run, see how they run,
They all ran after the farmer's wife,
She cut off their tails with a carving knife,
Did you ever see such a sight in your life,
As three blind mice.

Row, row, row your boat,
Gently down the stream
Merrily, merrily, merrily, merrily,
Life is but a dream.

Sweetly sings the donkey,
At the break of day.
If you do not feed him,
This is what he'll say:
Hee-haw! Hee-haw!
Hee-haw, hee-haw, hee-haw!

Are You Sleeping (Frère Jacques)

Are you sleeping, are you sleeping,
Brother John? Brother John?
Morning bells are ringing,
Morning bells are ringing
Ding, Ding, Dong,
Ding, Ding, Dong.

French version

Frère Jacques, frère Jacques,
Dormez vous? Dormez vous?
Sonnez les matines,
Sonnez les matines,
Din, Din, Don,
Din, Din, Don.

Note: Preschoolers cannot sing rounds. Sing these and
other rounds in unison.

OTHER FAMILIAR SONGS

Punchinello

What can you do Punchinello funny fellow,
What can you do Punchinello funny man?
(*Child in center makes a motion, and*
children in the circle copy motion and sing.)
We can do it too Punchinello funny fellow,
We can do it, too Punchinello funny man.

Jingle Bells

Jingle Bells. Jingle Bells.
Jingle all the way!
Oh what fun it is to ride in a one-horse open sleigh—
Jingle Bells. Jingle Bells.
Jingle all the way!
Oh what fun it is to ride in a one-horse open sleigh!

Yankee Doodle

Yankee Doodle went to town
A-riding on a pony.
He stuck a feather in his hat
And called it macaroni.

Chorus
Yankee Doodle, keep it up,
Yankee Doodle dandy,
Mind the music and the step,
And with the girls be handy.

Down by the Station

Down by the station early in the morning,
See the empty freight cars all in a row.
Hear the station master shouting "Load 'er up now!
"Load the train and off she'll go."

Have you loaded on the coal?
Yes, we've loaded on the coal.

Oh, down by the station early in the morning,
Hear the station master loadin' up the train.
Have you loaded on the trunks?
Yes we've loaded on the trunks.
And the coal?
And the coal.

List—pigs, cows, potatoes, etc.

Oh, down by the station early in the morning,
See the loaded freight cars all in a row.
Hear the station master shoutin' all aboard now,
Chug, chug, toot, toot; off we go.

I've Been Working On the Railroad

I've been working on the railroad all the livelong day,
I've been working on the railroad just to pass the time away.
Don't you hear the whistle blowing?
Rise up so early in the morn!
Don't you hear the captain shouting,
"Dinah blow your horn."
Dinah won't you blow? Dinah won't you blow?
Oh, Dinah won't you blow your horn, your horn.
Dinah won't you blow? Dinah won't you blow?
Oh, Dinah won't you blow your horn?

I See the Moon

I see the moon and the moon sees me.
The mocn sees the one that I want to see.
God bless the moon and God bless me.
And God bless the one that I want to see.

Pick a Bale of Cotton

You got to jump down, turn around
Pick a bale of cotton.
Jump down, turn around, Pick a bale a day.

Chorus
Oh lawdy, pick a bale of cotton
Oh lawdy, pick a bale a day.

Skip to My Lou

Flies in the buttermilk, shoo, fly, shoo
Flies in the buttermilk, shoo, fly, shoo,
Flies in the buttermilk, shoo, fly, shoo,
Skip to my Lou my darling.

Repeat, using (3 times):
Cat's in the cream jar, what'll I do?
Chicken's in the haystack, shoo, shoo, shoo.
Little red wagon painted blue.
Lost my sweetheart, what'll I do
I'll get another one prettier'n you.
Skip to my Lou my darling.

Oh Susanna

I come from Alabama with my banjo on my knee
I goin' to Lou'siana my Susanna for to see.
It rained all day the night I left
The weather was so dry
The sun so hot, I froze myself,
Susanna, don't you cry.

Chorus
Oh Susanna! Oh don't you cry for me,
For I come from Alabama
With my banjo on my knee.

Appendix 2

Activities Especially Suitable for Use by Fathers, Grandparents, Older Siblings and Sitters, Small Organized Groups

FATHERS

Block Bowling, 157
Box Houses, 152
Building and Floating Boats and
   Barges, 253
Drawing with Carbon Paper, 237
Explore the Neighborhood—What's
   Happening, 71
Leaf Pile Jump-up, 107
Paper Punching Bag, 180
Sand Block Musical Instruments,
   110
Shadow Show, 86
Sugar on Snow, 194
Table Hockey, 198
Trip to a Car Wash, 165
Tumbling Mattress, 138
Yes or No Animal Game, 226
Watching Popcorn Pop, 150

GRANDPARENTS

Baby Terrarium, 112
Beach Stone Games, 196
Birdseed Pictures in the Snow, 181
Button Book, 249
Collecting Seeds, 69
Company for Tea, 132

Cutting Snowflakes, 171
Going To See a Florist, 183
Nail Board, 141
Our Special Tree, 71
Pine Cone Tree, 148
Pine Needle Pillow, 62
Sawing Cardboard, 183
Sequence Puzzle Pictures, 244
Story of Me, 226
Transplanting Fun, 248

OLDER SIBLINGS AND SITTERS

Back in Order, 86
Be a Rubber Man, 112
Cranberry Relish, 106
Creative movement stories, 279
Do What I Do, 88
Fun with Scissors, 61
Hike in the House, 175
Magic Pictures with Crayon
   Rubbings, 81
Masking Tape Roads and Rooms, 84
Popsicle Stick Puppets, 176
Salt or Oatmeal Sandbox, 153
Shaving Cream Painting, 193
Trim Your Christmas Sandwich, 132
Whipping Snow, 173

SMALL ORGANIZED GROUPS

Appendix 3

Activities By Type

ARTS AND CRAFTS (*See* Part 1, 13-20, 27-39

Autumn tree, 77
BAKING CRYSTAL ORNAMENTS, 124
BIRDSEED PICTURES IN THE SNOW, 181
Bleach bottle pails and scoops, 233
BLOT MURAL, 80
Book marks, 37, 59, 213
BROWN BOTTLE VASE, 263
Brown paper tree, *Suggestion:* OUR SPECIAL TREE, 72
BUILDING AND FLOATING BOATS AND BARGES, 253
Bunnies: pictures, tuna can bunnies, 212
BURLAP GIFTS PAINTED WITH LOVE, 190
Burlap wall hanging, *Variation:* BURLAP GIFTS PAINTED WITH LOVE, 192
BUTTON BOOK, 249
CHILD'S AMERICAN FLAG, 266
CHRISTMAS TREE BELLS, 125
Clay: modeling, 38—39, 214
CLOTHESLINE ART SHOW, 236
CLOTHESPIN SAILBOAT, 236
Coloring book pages, 33—34
Contact paper activities, 38, 98, 213, 235, 192
Cut and paste activities, 36
  Acorns, 59
  Calendar numbers, 145
  Gift catalog activity, 122
  I Love You activity, 235
  Old cards, 98

  Seeds, 78
  Simple shapes, 28, 36
  Tearing and cutting, 35
  Variations: SCARY HOUSE, 91
CUTTING SNOWFLAKES, 171
DECORATE A SMALL TREE TO CHEER SOMEONE, 126
DECORATED SEA SHELLS OR STONES, 263
Decorating wastebaskets, canisters, boxes, 35
  Variations: VALENTINE MEMORIES TRAY, 172;
  Variation: PAINTING ON BURLAP, 192
Dot to dot drawing, *Variation:* PUNCHING HOLES AND SEWING, 172
DRAWING FROM LIFE, 215
DRAWING WITH CARBON PAPER, 237
DRIED ARRANGEMENTS IN HOLDERS, 102
Dried grasses, 97
Easter baskets, 214
Easter bunnies, 212
Easter hunt, 214
Egg carton animals, *Variations:* EGG CARTON BUTTERFLY, 239
EGG CARTON BUTTERFLY, 238
Eggs and eggshells, 19, 211
Envelopes, 169
Evergreens and pine needles, 97; Arrangements, 121
Fastening activity, 37
Feathers: collage, headbands, 59
"Feelies," *Variations:* FUZZY ANIMALS, 190
Finger painting, 27;

DRAMATIC PLAY (*See* Part 1, 45-46)

HOLIDAYS

FOR HOLIDAYS AND SPECIAL OCCASIONS
REFER TO THE PART 2 CONTENTS
PAGE FOR THE APPROPRIATE MONTH

MUSIC (*See* Part 1,16, 40-44; *See also* Appendix 1)